TROUBLESHOOTING FOR POTTERS

All the common problems, why they happen and how to fix them

Jacqui Atkin

APPLE

A QUARTO BOOK

First published in the UK in 2014 by
Apple Press
74–77 White Lion Street
London N1 9PF
UK

www.apple-press.com

ISBN: 978-1-8454-3549-3

QUAR: FIPO

Conceived, designed, and produced by
Quarto Publishing plc
The Old Brewery
6 Blundell Street
London N7 9BH

Project Editor: Chelsea Edwards
Designer: Austin Taylor
Photographer: Phil Wilkins
Illustrator: Kuo Kang Chen
Art Director: Caroline Guest
Copyeditor: Sarah Hoggett
Proofreader: Sally MacEachern
Indexer: Helen Snaith
Picture Researcher: Sarah Bell

Creative Director: Moira Clinch
Publisher: Paul Carslake

Colour separation in Singapore by
   Pica Digital Pte Limited
Printed in China by Hung Hing

9 8 7 6 5 4 3 2 1

Images: page 1 by Alistair Danhieux;
page 3 by Fenella Elms.

CONTENTS

Foreword	6
About this book	6

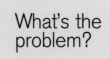

1 What's the problem?

What's the problem?	8
Diagnostic chart	9

2 Clays

Clays	34
BEST PRACTICE: The nature of clays	36
BEST PRACTICE: Clay particle orientation	41
FIX-ITS: Clay types: composition and nature	42
FIX-ITS: Clay preparation	52

| SPIRAL CRACKS | Fine cracks in thrown wares that spiral up from the base to follow the line of the form as it has been raised up from the wheel. | Overextending the clay by pulling up too quickly. | Increase the number of slightly slower speed. |
| **Applies to:** All clay types, especially throwing clays. | | Very marked throwing rings, creating thick and thin walls. | Use the sides of the fin upward to avoid making |

FORMING AND BISCUIT WARE – GENERAL FAULTS

PROBLEM	DESCRIPTION	CAUSES	FIX BY
EXPLOSIONS			
BLOW OUT **Applies to:** Any fired clay.	Fragments explode off the surface of biscuit-fired wares.	Almost always the result of clay contamination by lime, iron pyrites, etc.	Work away from areas Test-fire more of the cl appears to have come if making your own, che contaminants.
LIME POPPING **Applies to:** Most commonly, low-fired, grogged clay, but can occur in all clay types.	Small fragments flake away from the surface of biscuit-fired wares, leaving a cavity that typically has a white speck of lime-bearing material at its base.	Contamination by a lime-bearing substance such as concrete, plaster or limestone chipping.	Difficult to resolve – ch anyone else has had pr Check studio for possib check that it is not brea If mixing clay from dry dissolve small nodules. **Try also:** Reclaiming t slip stage. Test any nod hydrochloric acid – if th

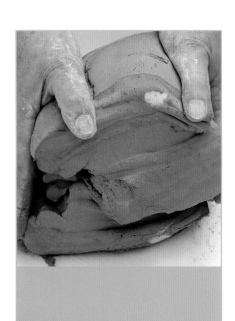

TROUBLESHOOTING
FOR POTTERS

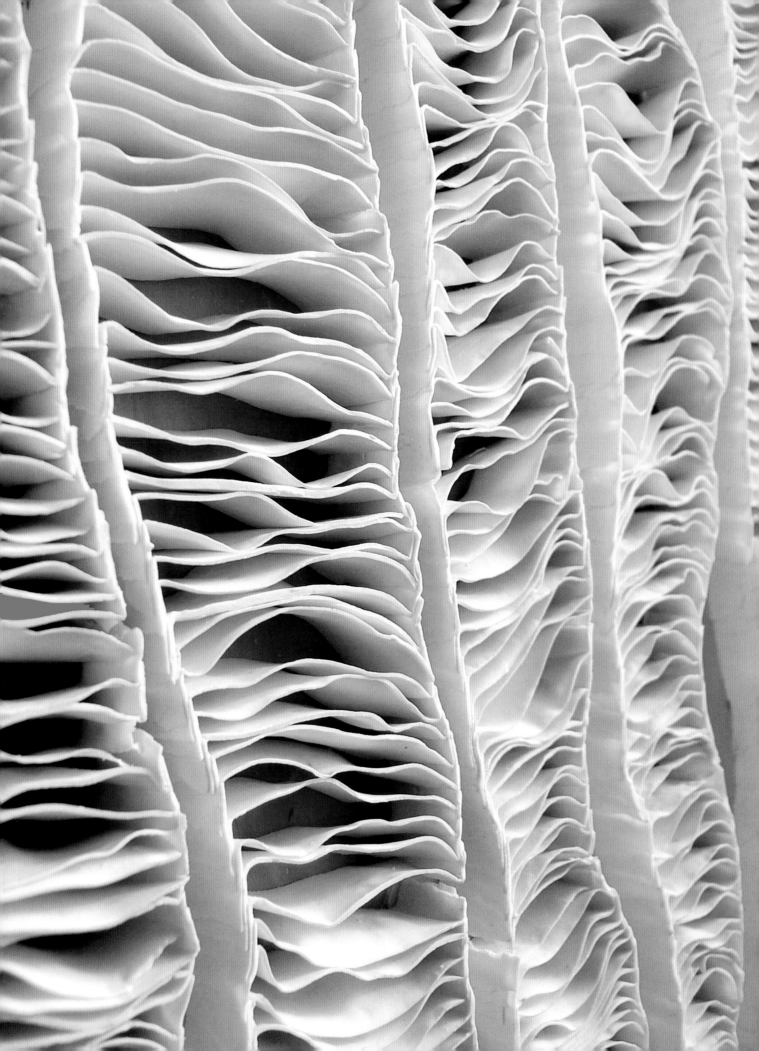

3 Forming and biscuit ware

Forming and biscuit ware	56
BEST PRACTICE: Forming	58
BEST PRACTICE: Drying considerations	66
FIX-ITS: Drying	67
FIX-ITS: Coiling	69
FIX-ITS: Pinching	70
FIX-ITS: Throwing	74
FIX-ITS: Turning	81
FIX-ITS: Slabbing	83
FIX-ITS: Slip casting	84

4 Surface decoration

Surface decoration	86
BEST PRACTICE: Surface decoration	88
BEST PRACTICE: Glazing	90
BEST PRACTICE: Colour and opacity in glazes	96
FIX-ITS: Slip and engobe faults	98
FIX-ITS: Glaze faults	103
FIX-ITS: Accidental reduction	107
FIX-ITS: Decorating faults	108
FIX-ITS: Last resort solutions	111

5 Firing

Firing	112
BEST PRACTICE: Firing	114
BEST PRACTICE: Kiln housekeeping	122
FIX-ITS: Low firing problems	124
FIX-ITS: Kilns: packing and firing	133

Health and safety	136
Glossary	136
Index	140
Credits	144

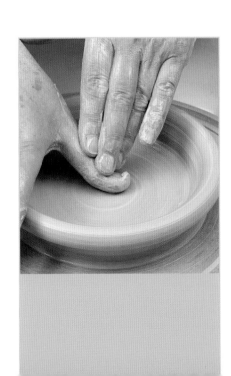

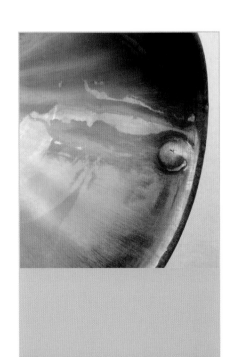

Foreword

The difficulty with writing a book of faults and remedies lies in the fact that many problems are maker specific – they arise out of certain working practices, affected by conditions in the studio perhaps, or firing methods. Added to this it can be difficult to define a fault because what one person may consider to be wrong can often be used by another for decorative effect – crawling and crazing are good examples of this. So, the solutions to problems can only be generic for the most part, given that individual circumstances cannot be known.

The purpose of this book is to provide the maker with a greater understanding of the ceramic process – from the basics of clay source, type and structure through all the stages of forming and decorating – so that problems can be avoided where possible. But, if they do arise, armed with a better understanding of process, the problem can be quickly identified and remedied.

The one thing to realize about working with clay is that it is a journey of discovery. It is actually important to make mistakes and for things to go wrong because we learn the most when we are challenged to think harder about our working practice. Also, it has to be said that often things may come out of the kiln not looking at all as we imagined they would, but better. In such cases a makers' signature is born.

So, don't be defeated by the things that go wrong, work through all the possible suggested remedies to rectify the problem and keep records. Make a diary of your working practice – clay type, making and drying methods, decorating and firing, etc., so that, if all else fails and you need more advice you will have all the information at hand.

J.P. Atkin.

About this book

Beginning with the diagnostic charts in Chapter One you can see at-a-glance where the root of your problem lies. Use the following four chapters to find the solution for whatever is preventing you from producing the work you want.

Chapter 1, pages 8–33

Twenty-five pages of diagnostic charts let you identify a specific problem, its cause and a solution, either directly from the chart, from the Fix-it part of the book or from the articles called Best Practice. Problems are organized into sections, based on the making process, and flagged to indicate the type of clay affected.

The colour-coded tabs help you to navigate the book's chapters.

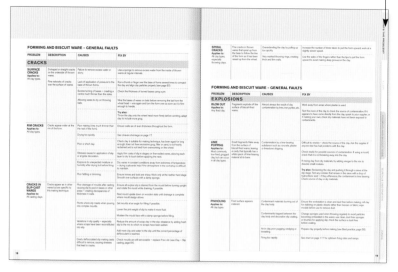

Potential causes are listed, often there is more than one.

Approaches for solving the problem.

The type of fault.

Label identifies the problem.

Describes how the problem looks and feels.

Chapters 2–5, pages 34–135

This content is organized into chapters linked to the key stages in the making process. Within each chapter are two types of content: Best Practice and Fix-its. Each chapter is introduced with Best Practice topics that help to lay the foundations for problem-free techniques. The Fix-it topics form the heart of each chapter. Here, faults are described in detail and causes discussed. Helpful solutions are offered.

Best practice-style article

Best practice articles describe the ideal way of working for each stage of the ceramic process.

Beautiful finished pieces are featured to demonstrate what can be achieved in each area.

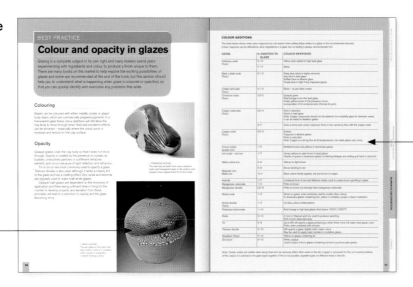

Charts are dotted throughout to provide at-a-glance reference points.

Fix-its-style article

The fix-its section of each chapter looks at the most common problems makers come across and describes approaches for troubleshooting.

Images of the faults aid easy diagnosis of the problem.

Specific solutions are suggested when a particular cause is known.

Photographs demonstrate the best ways to remedy the issue at hand.

CHAPTER 1
DIAGNOSTIC CHART

THE DIAGNOSTIC CHART IN THIS SECTION HAS BEEN DESIGNED AS A FIRST POINT OF REFERENCE AND IDENTIFIES MANY OF THE COMMON PROBLEMS THAT MAKERS COME UP AGAINST WHEN WORKING WITH CLAY. THE MAIN ISSUE IS TO RECOGNIZE WHERE YOU ARE GOING WRONG, SO SEVERAL OPTIONS FOR POSSIBLE CAUSES ARE LISTED, ALONG WITH SUGGESTIONS FOR WAYS TO REMEDY THE PROBLEM.

FORMING AND BISCUIT WARE – SPECIFIC FAULTS

PROBLEM	DESCRIPTION	CAUSES	FIX BY
CLAY			
CLAY TOO WET Applies to: All clay types.	Sticky, unworkable clay.	Incorrectly processed/reconstituted.	Spread over plaster bats – re-wedge to a workable consistency.
		Poor storage.	Store in dry, well-ventilated area without extremes of temperature or exposure to damp.
		Excessive organic content.	See below – clay too plastic. See solution for dry clay also.
CLAY TOO DRY Applies to: All clay types.	Hard clay with insufficient plasticity to work.	Poor storage.	See storage for wet clay – avoid exposure to heat.
		Exposure to heat/air.	**Try also:** Wedge with alternate layers of softer clay. Wrap clay in damp cloth, seal in plastic bag for 24 hours. Pierce holes through the bag the clay is contained in, submerge in a bucket of water for 30 minutes, then seal in a second bag for 24 hours.
CLAY NOT PLASTIC ENOUGH Applies to: All clay types.	Clay handles poorly. Lacks malleability (is short). Cracks easily.	Clay particle size most directly affects plasticity.	See Best practice, page 41.
		Ratio of water to dry clay insufficient.	Either reclaim or wedge with softer clay for a more workable body.
		Poorly prepared clay.	If mixing your own clay body – blunge clay for a longer period to break it down.
		Reconstituted clay – lack of maturing time before use.	Leave to mature for 4–10 weeks after reclaiming.
		Water pH when mixing clay – too acidic.	Use water with mild acidity – pH 6.5 for best results (tap water). **Try also:** Adding ball clay. Using a more plastic kaolin. Decreasing nonplastic additions. Adding 1–2% bentonite.
CLAY TOO PLASTIC (FAT CLAY) Applies to: All clay types.	Clay excessively sticky. Clay is hard to work. High shrinkage.	Excessive amounts of carbonaceous or organic matter in the clay.	Add coarser clays (nonplastic kaolins, fireclay) or add other nonplastic ingredients (see Best practice, page 36).
AIR IN THE CLAY Applies to: All clay types.	Air bubbles in clay evident when making.	Poorly prepared clay.	Process clay through a de-airing pug mill. Wedge the clay thoroughly before use. Wedge properly to avoid introducing air (see Best practice, page 58).

PROBLEM	DESCRIPTION	CAUSES	FIX BY
FUNGAL GROWTH IN OR ON THE CLAY **Applies to:** All clay types.	Green/black mould on the surface or in clay. Can be smelly!	Exposing clay to moisture.	Simply wedge or knead the mould into the clay; it will aid plasticity.
		Storing clay for too long.	Store clay in a dry place away from extremes of temperature.
		Homemade paper clay.	Add a capful of bleach to the water when making the clay – use the clay quickly – avoid storing for long periods.
		Using non-tap/stored or dirty water to reclaim.	Use tap water or add a capful of bleach to the water.
WEDGING AND KNEADING **Applies to:** All clay types.	Air introduced in the process.	Using incorrect wedging or kneading technique.	See page 53 for correct techniques for wedging and kneading.
	Contamination from other materials.	Preparing the clay in a contaminated area – near plaster, or in an area where clay of another colour has been prepared.	Make sure the preparation area is spotlessly clean, free from dust and never near an area where plaster is used. Never process white clays in the same area as red clays. See page 53 for correct technique.

FORMING AND BISCUIT WARE – SPECIFIC FAULTS

PROBLEM	DESCRIPTION	CAUSES	FIX BY
CLAY: HAND-BUILDING			
SPLITTING SEAMS **Applies to:** Coiling, slabbing, pinching.	Wares split along seams that have been joined together.	Poor scoring of edges.	Score edges using an old toothbrush and water to really roughen the surface.
		Insufficient lubrication.	Try using slip made from the same clay.
		Lack of/poor reinforcement to joins.	Reinforce internal joins with thin coils of soft clay where possible.
		Drying too quickly/unevenly.	Dry wares slowly, away from extremes of heat or draughts. See Best practice, page 66.
UNEVEN DRYING **Applies to:** Coiling, modelling/ sculpting, and most other hand-building methods.	Warped shape. Cracks.	Drying wares too quickly.	Cover items with light plastic and allow to dry slowly unless the facility for humidity drying is available. Place wares on a wire rack to allow the undersides to dry at the same rate.
		Exposing wares to a heat source on one side.	Dry in an area of consistent temperature away from direct sources of heat (even the sun).
		Exposing wares to draughts.	Keep wares away from open doors or windows.
		Wares with uneven thickness in the clay walls.	Make sure the thickness of clay wall is even throughout, including the base. See Best practice, page 66.

DISTORTED SHAPE **Applies to:** Coiling, pinching, slabbing.	Wares distort or warp as they dry – may be more evident after biscuit firing. Tiles are especially problematic.	Poor making technique – uneven thickness in the clay wall.	Dry and fire items of uneven thickness very, very slowly but where possible construct to ensure walls are of even thickness.
		Drying flat.	Dry tiles upright, stacked together, separating each one with pellets of soft clay to allow air movement between. Make allowance for clay memory.
		Poor clay choice for making technique – clay too fine for task.	Use grogged clay or incorporate grog into the clay to give greater warp resistance. Coarse grog gives the best effect, but for a finer surface use 100 dust grog or fine sand.
		Drying wares too quickly. Exposing wares to a heat source on one side. Exposing wares to draughts. Wares with uneven thickness in the clay walls.	See also Kiln housekeeping, page 122, for best ways to pack kilns to avoid warping and distortion.
COLLAPSING SHAPE **Applies to:** All hand-building methods.	Shape begins to sag as it is constructed.	Weight of clay.	Build walls as thin as the form will allow for support and keep an even thickness throughout.
		Clay too wet.	Firm the clay up periodically – using a hairdryer – turning the form continuously to avoid overdrying.
		Clay not fit for purpose – wrong for the forming technique.	Use grogged clay for large or complex constructions/sculpture; finer clays for smaller constructions that need less support.
SURFACE CRACKING **Applies to:** Coiling, slabbing, pinching.	Tiny, vein-like cracks over the surface of the clay – especially evident when pinching but can be seen in some other hand-building techniques.	Hot hands.	Cool hands in cold water periodically.
		Firm clay.	For pinching and coiling work with softer clay – use a hairdryer to firm the clay up at appropriate stages of construction.
		Wrong clay.	Choose clay suitable for technique (see Clay types: composition and nature, page 42).
UNEVEN CLAY WALLS **Applies to:** Hand-building methods. See also: Uneven walls and rims in the throwing section.	Lumpy, bulging clay surface. Poor shape definition.	Poor making technique.	Refine the surface of the wares at regular intervals using a metal kidney to scrape away excess clay. Use an outline former to keep the shape true. Measure the thickness of the walls at intervals using a pin.

FORMING AND BISCUIT WARE – SPECIFIC FAULTS

PROBLEM	DESCRIPTION	CAUSES	FIX BY
CLAY: THROWING			
AIR IN CLAY **Applies to:** All clay types and other making methods.	Air bubbles in the clay becoming more noticeable as the form is refined.	Poor clay preparation.	Thoroughly wedge and knead clay before use (see Best practice, page 58). Use a pin to deflate bubbles.
UNEVEN WALLS AND RIMS **Applies to:** All clay types.	Clay feels uneven as it is being raised up. Thick and thin areas on the rim. Uneven rim.	Badly centred clay.	Practise correct centring.
		Poorly prepared wheel head.	Correct problems with the wheel head.
		Poorly prepared clay.	Wedge clay well, form into appropriately sized balls ready for use and keep prepared clay under plastic until ready to use.
		Knocking off-centre.	Remove hands carefully by throwing beyond the pot, as though it is taller than it really is.
		Insufficient use of water (dry hands).	Increase the amount of water used to raise the form. Keep hands wet but mop up excess periodically.
		Poor working position.	Correct posture. **Try also:** Remove uneven rims using a pin or knife positioned just below the ragged edge while the wheel is turning.
COLLAPSING FORMS **Applies to:** All clay types.	Form collapses as it is raised. Cylinders collapse when closing in.	Unsuitable clay.	Choose clay that is suitable for the type of work (see Clay types: composition and nature, page 42). Firmer clays hold their shape better.
		Saturation or use of too much water.	Minimize amount of water used and mop up excess regularly.
		Overworking the form.	Complete the pot in fewer moves.
		Air bubbles.	Thoroughly wedge and knead clay before use (see Best practice, page 58).
		Undermining – too narrow base.	Leave enough clay width at the base of the form to support weight as it is raised.
		Wall too thin.	Increase the thickness of the clay wall.
		Inconsistencies in thickness of clay wall.	Test in increments to find the best thickness for the clay type and style of form.
		Overthinning of walls with too much weight at the top of the form.	Keep the walls slightly too thick until the form is almost complete, then refine so thickness and weight are even throughout the process.

PROBLEM	DESCRIPTION	CAUSES	FIX BY
TEAPOT SPOUT AND HANDLE TWIST **Applies to:** All clay types.	Spouts and handles appear twisted after firing.	Wrong type of clay.	Avoid very soft clay – firm the clay prior to throwing by kneading on a plaster bat to remove excess moisture. See Firming clay for wedging, page 52.
		Working technique – clay spiral unravels in firing.	Adopt a quick throwing style for spouts – overworking causes the clay to twist in firing.
		Firing temperature – most problematical with higher firings.	Experiment with lower-firing clays with similar qualities to the one being used: for instance a white-firing earthenware or mid-range clay to replace a white stoneware. **Try also:** Make test pieces to measure twist then adapt application accordingly.
COMPONENT PARTS CRACKING AND BREAKING APART **Applies to:** All clay types.	Handles, spouts or lids crack or break off the form.	Stress – a difference between the hardness of clay in body and component part.	Make all parts of the form together and join while all are at the same stage of hardness.
		Poor joining.	Use slip made from the same clay body. Make sure that both surfaces to be joined have been scored and that sufficient slip is used to secure both together.
		Draughts (rapid, uneven drying).	Dry forms away from direct heat or draughts. Component parts will dry faster than the body so cover with loose plastic to allow all to dry at the same speed.
		Different clay bodies.	Check you are using the same clay for component parts as for the main body – even using clay from a new bag can have some effect.
		Rough handling, distorting shape.	Support work to which parts are added to avoid distorting shape – use hands to support interiors and foam or sponge to rest larger items on.

FORMING AND BISCUIT WARE: SPECIFIC FAULTS

PROBLEM	DESCRIPTION	CAUSES	FIX BY
CLAY: SLIP CASTING			
MOULD WON'T RELEASE **Applies to:** All casting clay types.	Cast form will not release from the mould.	Undercuts.	Remodel the shape to remove undercuts – recast the form in plaster. **Try also:** Sanding the undercut away from the plaster mould (only possible if not too deep); wear a dust mask and work away from clay.
		Excess deflocculant in slip.	Add a trace of flocculent to the slip (try vinegar). Or add more water and clay to the slip in stages until the correct per centage of deflocculant is achieved.
		Worn moulds.	Try dusting the mould surface with talcum powder. Sponge off before using.
MOULD STAINING **Applies to:** Plaster moulds.	A dark brown stain on the mould that gets progressively worse with use, causing casts to stick.	Excess deflocculant in slip.	Decant the brown liquid seen floating on the top of slips where possible and replace with fresh slip.
			Mix faulty slip with good slip in small measures until used up to avoid wastage.

Problem	Symptoms	Cause	Solution
SLIP DIFFICULT TO POUR OFF – BAD DRAINING **Applies to:** All casting clay types.	Moulds are difficult to empty of slip after casting.	Under-deflocculated slip.	Add a very small amount of water to correct fluidity or adjust with a drop or two of sodium silicate. Ask your supplier about slip-testing kits, which should include a viscometer to measure the viscosity of slip.
		Excess deflocculant in slip (slip gets thicker if excess deflocculant is present).	Test a sample of slip by adding a few drops of sodium silicate – if the slip thickens, it already has too much deflocculant. **Try also:** Check the pint weight of the slip (clay to water ratio) – the heavier the slip the slower the run off. See page 65 for measuring pint weight.
SLOW CASTING **Applies to:** All casting slips.	Items take too long to cast.	Fluidity is too high.	Reduce water content.
		Thixotropy too low.	Increase alkali addition to slip.
PINHOLING **Applies to:** All casting clays.	Small holes in the surface of cast wares (on the mould side of the cast).	Dust/dirt on mould surface or falling into stored slip.	Wipe moulds with a barely damp cloth before casting. Store slip in a sealed container away from contaminants.
		Fluidity too low.	Increase water addition.
		New moulds.	Discard the first cast from a new mould – subsequent casts should be better.
		Using reclaimed slip.	Only return slip to the main stock if sure it is contaminant-free, otherwise re-blunge for safety.
		Poor blunging – introducing air into slip.	Make sure the blunger blades are below the surface of the slip. Increase blunging time.
		Using slip directly from the blunger.	If possible after blunging, sieve slip into an agitator to remove air. If possible, allow slip to stand overnight.
WREATHING **Applies to:** All casting clays.	Small uneven ridges, lines or corrugations on the sides of cast wares.	Thixotropy too low.	Decrease the alkali addition to the slip.
		Draining slip unevenly (can be a problem with slips with a fast casting rate e.g. bone china).	Drain evenly and steadily, turning the mould in the process if possible.
		Semi-saturated moulds.	Allow moulds to dry thoroughly between castings.
		Moulds in poor condition.	Replace old moulds.

Problem	Description	Cause	Solution
CASTING SPOT **Applies to:** All casting clays.	Dense vitreous areas where the slip first impacts onto the mould. May also present as a discoloured mark on the cast after firing and cause problems with glaze application as vitrification occurs at this spot.	Thixotropy too low.	Reduce alkali addition to slip.
		Separation of clay particles when the slip hits the mould, causing mica particles (which are flat) to align in one direction.	Pour slip into the mould as near to the feed hole as possible and drain through a conical sieve. Pour the slip into the mould so that it hits the base or a less-important part first. **Try also:** Sponge the mould with a thin layer of slip if the problem is really bad.
PROMINENT JOIN MARKS **Applies to:** All casting clays.	Evident only after firing: Ridges protruding from the cast form when mould sections joined.	Large gaps in mould joints, causing problems with particle alignment.	Undercut joins at the fettling stage of casting so that they fire flush (tricky to do successfully). Try a slip with less clay and more filler. Replace worn moulds and ensure close fit of joins.
FLABBY CASTS **Applies to:** All casting clays.	Casts distort easily when handling.	Thixotropy too high.	Lower alkali content of slip.
BRITTLE CASTS **Applies to:** All casting clays.	Surface of the cast is hard and difficult to cut and fettle.	Thixotropy too low.	Increase alkali content of slip.
LIVERING **Applies to:** All casting slips.	Surface of the slip has the appearance of wet liver (i.e. jelly-like and thick).	Slip has stood too long (over-exposure to air).	Store slip in airtight containers when not being used.
		Under deflocculation.	Check pint weight and correct (see page 65).
		Excessive use of sodium silicate.	Reduce amount of sodium silicate.
		Very hard water/soluble salts.	Decrease alkali – use water from another source if possible.
		Plaster contamination.	Avoid contamination by working away from the area where plaster is used. Make sure plaster does not break away from moulds when pouring out slip.
LAMINATED CASTS **Applies to:** Most commonly, slips containing a single-fire clay but can happen in all types.	Manifests as two distinct textures or colours in the walls or base of casts, leading to structural failure.	The coarsest fraction of the slip separates and casts first, leaving finer particles to cast above.	Work at a higher pint weight (see page 65). **Try also:** Adjust the slip mix by adding a ball clay or very plastic fireclay with significant colloidal material – ask your supplier for suitable types.

FORMING AND BISCUIT WARE – GENERAL FAULTS

PROBLEM	DESCRIPTION	CAUSES	FIX BY
CLAY			
LOW GREEN STRENGTH **Applies to:** White earthenware. Some highly grogged stonewares. Porcelain.	Clay is difficult to work. Clay won't hold its shape. Poor throwing qualities. Collapses easily.	Poor clay constituents.	Replace one ball clay, fireclay or china clay with another addition of highly plastic ball clay.
		Clay particle size – grogs, sands.	Check particle size by sieve testing and adjust accordingly.
		Insufficient ageing – poor weathering.	Allow a longer maturing time – 6–10 weeks.
		Newly made clay or reclaimed clay.	Lengthen blunging time when mixing clay.
		Insufficiently de-aired clay.	Put clay through a de-airing pug mill.
		Handling the ware at its most vulnerable stage.	Retard drying time to allow handling at the leather-hard stage, not the dry stage. **Try also:** Add bentonite to the clay mix. Add fibrous material such as paper pulp, nylon fibre or horsehair.
SCUMMING **Applies to:** Predominantly red clays, but occurs also with earthenware, stoneware and porcelain.	Deposits on the surface and especially the edges of dry or fired wares.	Excess of soluble salts in the clay.	Add 0.5–2.5% barium carbonate to clay before blunging. Barium carbonate can be expensive, but it's very useful when adding earth materials like ochres to clay in large amounts.
		Clay production methods – especially clay made in dough mixers, pan mills and so on.	Buy clay produced by the slip-housing method.
		Rapid drying.	Slow down drying time to allow the scum to be more evenly dispersed and reduce concentration at edges.
		Salts introduced in water supply from static tanks where water is subject to evaporation.	Check water source – mains supply or drinking water is the best choice. **Try also:** Dry wares upside down so that deposits form on the underside where it matters less.
SPECKING **Applies to:** All clay types.	Unwanted specks in the fired clay body – may be present only on the surface or in the actual body. Specks may affect glaze.	Contamination of clay at the manufacturing or making stage.	Specks on both interior and exterior surfaces of wares indicate a clay manufacture problem – speak to your supplier if buying ready-made clay, or check your ingredients for contaminants if making yourself. Be particularly aware of contamination from the rust from metal containers as well as placing sand and bits of brick.

FORMING AND BISCUIT WARE – GENERAL FAULTS

PROBLEM	DESCRIPTION	CAUSES	FIX BY
DRYING			
UNEVEN SHRINKAGE **Applies to:** All clay types.	Distortion of shape, manifesting in either the dry ware or after biscuit firing.	Poor shaping method.	Avoid distortion of form at the making stage – understand clay memory.
		Uneven drying.	Dry away from extremes of heat or cold.
		Predominant heat source in drying.	Ensure the drying area allows free movement of air around the form. Drying on slatted racks will help flow of air. Avoid draughts or heat sources to specific sides of wares.
		Clay plate orientation.	Understand plate orientation (see page 41).
		Uneven thickness in clay walls.	Ensure the clay walls are of even thickness. **Try also:** Turn the form frequently as it dries.
WARPING **Applies to:** All clay types.	Wares distort as they dry becoming more obvious after firing.	Poor making technique.	Ensure walls are of even thickness – scrape back regularly and check thickness with a pin periodically. Dry and fire wares very slowly.
		Poor drying technique.	For flat or heavy items, dry on paper or fine sand placed over the drying rack. See Uneven shrinkage, above.
		Wrong clay.	Check the clay being used is suitable for purpose – the greater amount of grog in the clay, the better the warpage resistance.
		Mishandling wares/clay memory.	Where possible avoid excessive handling before the leather-hard stage or when completely dry. See Clay particle orientation on page 41 and Clay types: composition and nature on page 42.
		Design.	Avoid large flat areas where possible – structure the design to facilitate movement in the shape as a feature.
		Bad support when firing/poor kiln packing.	See Kiln housekeeping on page 122 for placing/setting methods.
		Firing speed.	See Firing charts on page 117 for optimum firing ramps and rates.

FORMING AND BISCUIT WARE – GENERAL FAULTS

PROBLEM	DESCRIPTION	CAUSES	FIX BY
CRACKS			
SURFACE CRACKS Applies to: All clay types.	S-shaped or straight cracks on the underside of thrown wares. Fine networks of cracks over the surface of wares.	Failure to remove excess water or slurry.	Use a sponge to remove excess water from the inside of thrown wares at regular intervals.
		Lack of application of pressure to the base of thrown forms.	Run a thumb or finger over the base of forms several times to compact the clay and align clay particles properly (see page 80).
		Excess turning of bases – creating a centre much thinner than the sides.	Check the thickness of turned bases using a pin.
		Allowing wares to dry on throwing bats.	Wire the bases of wares on bats before removing the bat from the wheel head – wire again and turn the form over as soon as it is firm enough to handle.
			Try also: Throw the clay onto the wheel head more firmly before centring; adapt clay to include more grog.
RIM CRACKS Applies to: All clay types.	Cracks appear wider at the rim of the form.	Poor making (rims much thinner than the rest of the form).	Ensure walls are of even thickness throughout the form.
		Drying too quickly.	See Uneven shrinkage on page 17.
		Poor or short clay.	Check clay is suitable for making technique, has been aged for long enough, does not have excessive grog, filler or sand, is not freshly reclaimed and is not tired from overworking on the wheel.
		Stresses caused in application of slip or engobe decoration.	Apply thin coats of slip in stages on fine-walled wares, allowing each layer to dry to touch before applying the next.
		Exposure to unexpected moisture or humidity after drying but before firing.	Dry wares in constant conditions away from extremes of temperature – drying cupboards help if the atmosphere in the workshop is difficult to maintain.
		Poor fettling or trimming.	Ensure knives and tools are sharp. Work only at the leather-hard stage Smooth over surfaces with a damp sponge.
CRACKS IN SLIP-CAST WARES Applies to: All casting clays.	Cracks appear as in other wares but are specific to this making technique.	Poor drainage of moulds after casting causing slip to pool in bases or other areas – creating discrepancies of thickness in walls.	Ensure all surplus slip is drained from the mould before turning upright and rotate the mould while draining, if possible. Rest mould upside down on wooden slats until drainage is complete where mould design allows.
		Points where slip meets when pouring into complex moulds.	Set moulds at an angle for filling if possible. Lower the pint weight of slip to make it more fluid. Moisten the mould face with a damp sponge before filling.
		Variations in slip quality – especially where scraps have been reconstituted into slip.	Reduce the amount of scrap clay in the slip; rebalance by adding fresh slip to the mix to which no scraps have been added. Add more clay and water to the slip until the correct percentage of deflocculant is reached.
		Overly deflocculated slip making casts difficult to remove, causing stresses that lead to cracks.	Check moulds are still serviceable – replace if too old. (see Clay – Slip casting, page 84).

SPIRAL CRACKS **Applies to:** All clay types, especially throwing clays.	Fine cracks in thrown wares that spiral up from the base to follow the line of the form as it has been raised up from the wheel.	Overextending the clay by pulling up too quickly.	Increase the number of times taken to pull the form upward; work at a slightly slower speed.
		Very marked throwing rings, creating thick and thin walls.	Use the sides of the fingers rather than the tips to pull the form upward to avoid making deep grooves in the clay.

FORMING AND BISCUIT WARE – GENERAL FAULTS

PROBLEM	DESCRIPTION	CAUSES	FIX BY
EXPLOSIONS			
BLOW OUT **Applies to:** Any fired clay.	Fragments explode off the surface of biscuit-fired wares.	Almost always the result of clay contamination by lime, iron pyrites, etc.	Work away from areas where plaster is used. Test-fire more of the clay to check the source of contamination. If it appears to have come directly from the clay, speak to your supplier, or if making your own, check dry materials have not been exposed to contaminants.
LIME POPPING **Applies to:** Most commonly, low-fired, grogged clay, but can occur in all clay types.	Small fragments flake away from the surface of biscuit-fired wares, leaving a cavity that typically has a white speck of lime-bearing material at its base.	Contamination by a lime-bearing substance such as concrete, plaster or limestone chipping.	Difficult to resolve – check the source of the clay. Ask the supplier if anyone else has had problems with the clay. Check studio for possible sources of contamination. If using a mould, check that it is not breaking away into the clay. If mixing clay from dry materials, try adding vinegar to the mix to dissolve small nodules. **Try also:** Reclaiming the clay and pushing it through a sieve at the slip stage. Test any nodules that remain in the sieve with a drop of hydrochloric acid – if they effervesce, the contaminant is lime bearing. Check source of clay or dry materials.
PINHOLING **Applies to:** All clay types.	Fired surface appears cratered.	Contaminant materials burning out of the clay body.	Ensure the workstation is clean and dust-free before making; roll clay for slabbing on plastic sheets rather than hessian or fabric; wipe moulds before use to remove dust.
		Contaminants trapped between the clay body and decorative slip coating.	Change sponges used when throwing regularly to avoid particles becoming embedded in the wares; use clean, dust-free sponges or brushes for applying slip; check the surface is dust-free before coating.
		Air in clay, poor pugging, wedging or kneading.	Prepare clay properly before making (see Best practice, page 58).
		Firing too rapidly.	See chart on page 117 for optimum firing rates and ramps.

BLOATING AND BLISTERING **Applies to:** All clay types.	Swollen, bloated bubbles appear to be trapped beneath the clay surface (seen most generally in vitrified and glazed wares).	Large bubbles caused by expanding gases trapped in the clay by firing too quickly.	Slow down the firing speed between 600°C (1112°F) and 1000°C (1832°F) to 100°C (212°F) per hour. **Try also:** Soak at 1000°C (1832°F) for an hour to compensate for over-fast firing.
	Fine bubbling at the surface.	Over-firing.	Reduce the top temperature – regulate the firing ramp. Test-fire the kiln to ensure it is working properly. Check clay is being fired to recommended temperature.
		With red-firing clays, a reduction atmosphere in the kiln at a stage in the firing ramp when volatiles are burning away.	Pack the kiln more loosely to allow free movement of air around wares; ensure free movement of air through the kiln while volatiles are burning away (up to 1000°C/1832°F); put bungs in at a later stage. **Try also:** Using a more-grogged body.
LOW FIRED STRENGTH **Applies to:** All fired clays.	Fragile wares lacking durability.	Under-firing or firing too quickly.	Check the clay is firing to recommended temperature at correct rate (see Firing chart, page 117). Check the kiln is not too densely packed – this can prevent some wares from firing correctly. Check kiln elements are all working if firing electric.
		Wares too thin.	Increase the thickness of the clay wall a little; cast mould-made items for a shorter time.
		Additions of too much grog or filler in the clay.	Wedge ungrogged clay into the mix to reduce quantity and refine the body.
		Overly reconstituted clay.	Mix reconstituted clay 50:50 with new clay to make a more durable body. Allow reclaimed clay to mature for 4–10 weeks before using.
		Poor clay preparation.	De-air clay thoroughly before using – put through a de-airing pug mill if possible, otherwise wedge thoroughly.
		Poor design – sharp, angled forms.	Think about the vulnerability of a shape before making – modify design to make fit for purpose. Soften sharp angles where possible to reduce vulnerability to knocking and chipping.
		Diminished flux content in clay.	Test-fire samples to compare with previously satisfactory clay. Check source of clay. Overly reclaimed can have the effect of leaching out vital materials – mix with new clay to regulate content.
GENERAL EXPLOSIONS **Applies to:** All clay types.	Large areas blasted away from the surface of wares or complete shattering.	Firing wares before they are fully dry. Firing too rapidly over the first 250°C (482°F).	Dry wares out completely before firing, or fire extremely slowly, allowing good ventilation over the first phase of firing.

SURFACE DECORATION – GENERAL FAULTS

PROBLEM	DESCRIPTION	CAUSES	FIX BY
SLIPS AND ENGOBES			
FLAKING ON GREENWARE Applies to: All clay types.	Slip curls away from surfaces and drops off.	Discrepancy in rate of shrinkage between slip and clay body.	For slip that has a high shrinkage, apply a thinner coat. Add 10–20% fine molochite, sand, grog, quartz or calcined alumina to the slip. Check the ball clay content of the slip is correct – it needs to be a low-shrinkage variety.
		Applying slip at the wrong stage.	Apply the slip at an earlier stage – when the pot is still leather hard or sooner if possible. Dry the ware more slowly. **Try also:** Deflocculating the slip by adding a few drops of sodium silicate. Stirring the slip well before use to check the filler content has not settled at the bottom. For slip with too low shrinkage (not common), apply slip to drier wares. Add 1–5% bentonite or ball clay to the slip. Add gum arabic to the slip to help it to stick. Reduce content of grog to slip.
FLAKING ON BISCUIT WARE Applies to: All clay types, but most commonly red earthenware.	Flaking along rims and convex surfaces – often only after glaze firing.	Difference in firing shrinkage of slip and clay body.	Add 20% of the covering glaze to the slip mixture before application. Replace slip content with feldspar, Cornish stone, nepheline syenite or other alternative fluxes instead of quartz, flint or china clay – if this exacerbates the problem – reverse the above.

SURFACE DECORATION – GENERAL FAULTS

PROBLEM	DESCRIPTION	CAUSES	FIX BY
GLAZE PREPARATION			
GLAZE TOO THICK Applies to: All glaze mixes.	Glaze doesn't run off when applied to wares.	Insufficient water content when mixing.	Use more water when mixing – if necessary, decant off excess later to correct consistency.
		Constant use on porous biscuit ware reducing water content.	If glazing from a large vat, use a hydrometer to check the glaze consistency periodically and correct by adding water.
GLAZE SETTLEMENT Applies to: All glaze mixes.	Glaze ingredients settled in the bottom of the bucket – difficult to mix.	Weight of glaze ingredients.	Add 1% bentonite to the dry ingredients before mixing the glaze.
		Lack of use/settlement over time.	Alternatively, try adding a flocculent – calcium chloride, calcium sulphate or magnesium sulphate.
		Glaze stored in metal containers.	Store glaze in plastic or wooden containers only.

SURFACE DECORATION – GENERAL FAULTS

PROBLEM	DESCRIPTION	CAUSES	FIX BY
GLAZE APPLICATION			
FINGER MARKS Applies to: All glazes applied by hand methods.	Obvious finger marks in the fired glaze – finger-shaped areas where glaze appears not to have covered the surface.	Application method.	Cover finger marks by dabbing glaze over the finger mark using either a finger or glaze mop. Smooth the surface back to match the surrounding glaze. Use a glaze claw for dipping. Design the shape to allow for handling when dipping.
UNEVEN GLAZE – THICK AND THIN AREAS Applies to: All glaze application methods, but most common in coloured glazes.	Glaze appears thicker and brighter in some areas, often showing crystal growth, and thinner in others, especially obvious over darker-firing bodies.	Application methods.	Avoid pouring unless an overlapped surface is required. Spray where possible. Choose an opaque glaze rather than a transparent glaze.
		Type of glaze – addition of texturing agents to glaze like ilmenite or rutile.	Test the glaze to find the required surface quality.
		Discrepancies in porosity of the biscuit ware – occurring in firing.	Position wares away from kiln elements for more even firing.
		Uneven firing.	Avoid overloading kiln and fire more slowly.
GLAZE WON'T ADHERE TO BISCUIT SURFACE Applies to: All glazes.	Glaze runs off the surface instead of adhering.	Biscuit fire too high – clay has vitrified.	Reduce the biscuit firing temperature. Check the kiln is firing correctly.
		Wares too thin.	Apply glaze in two thin coats, allowing each layer to dry thoroughly between coats. **Try also:** Add a flocculent to the glaze – calcium chloride or magnesium sulphate.
CHITTERED EDGES WHEN USING SGRAFFITO THROUGH GLAZE Applies to: All glazes.	Glaze crawls where the sgraffito lines have been scratched, or falls away completely.	Type of glaze used – matt varieties are worse.	Use the technique with a more liquid type of glaze that will melt more readily. Alternatively, fill the sgraffito lines with another, contrasting glaze.
PAINTBRUSH ADHERES TO THE SURFACE Applies to: All glazes applied by this method.	Application almost impossible because the brush sticks to the surface.	Porous clay sucking water from the brush.	Use a dense glaze brush to allow sufficient glaze to be carried for a full brush stroke. Work on a banding wheel for quick and even application.
		Using incorrect glazing method.	Use another method like dipping, pouring or spraying for overall application. Use brushing for glaze-on-glaze decoration instead.
		Glaze too thick or too thin.	Test the glaze with a hydrometer for optimum use. Practise the technique on test pieces before committing to best wares.

TRAILING – GLAZE RUNS OFF THE SURFACE **Applies to:** Multiple glaze applications.	Glaze used in the same way as for slip trailing won't adhere or runs off vertical surfaces.	Glaze too thin.	Reduce the water content when mixing glaze or if ready mixed heat the glaze to drive off water.
		Biscuit has been fired too high – clay body not porous enough.	Reduce the biscuit firing temperature – check wares are not too close to elements. See chart on page 117 for optimum firing rates and ramps.
RAW/GREEN GLAZING – COLLAPSING FORMS **Applies to:** Any clay forms glazed in this way.	Forms fall apart or component parts fall off after glazing.	Oversaturation of clay.	Glaze quickly and efficiently – do not allow glaze to linger inside a form. Glaze inside first – allow to dry before glazing exterior.
		Glazing at the wrong stage.	Test clay at various stages of dryness to find the optimum time for glazing your clay.
		Wrong glaze/glaze too thin.	Adjust glaze to include at least 25% clay content. Raw glaze must be thicker than normal – add carboxymethyl cellulose to glaze intended for use on dry pots.
		Overhandling the wares – lifting by handles, etc.	Lift wares at a point to cause least stress: never by the handles. Try dusting dry glaze onto wetter, more open surfaces like plates or bowls. Apply through a fine sieve, and make sure to wear a dust mask.

SURFACE DECORATION – GENERAL FAULTS

PROBLEM	DESCRIPTION	CAUSES	FIX BY
GLAZE: FAULTS IN FIRED SURFACES			
DUNTING **Applies to:** All clay types.	A crack that runs completely through the fired body.	Most commonly stress in firing – either heating too quickly or cooling too quickly – or over-firing.	Slow down both firing speed and cooling speed. Leave bungs in after firing and don't open the kiln until a handling temperature is reached. See page 117 for correct firing ramps and rates. Raise wares from the kiln shelf on supports if possible and suitable for clay type.
		Poor design – cracking from corners or angles. Shape of wares/uneven thickness in sections.	Smooth over angles and holes cut into the clay body at the making stage with a damp sponge.
		Use of smooth-bodied, dense clay.	Lower the firing temperature and apply a lower firing glaze, or open up the clay body by adding grog.
		Glaze thickness.	Do not allow liquid glaze to pool in the bottom of wares, keep inverted until all excess has drained away. Use a thinner glaze covering.
		Glaze/body fit – glaze with high craze resistance used on body with wide firing range.	Choose a clay type more specific to firing requirements and adjust glaze to suit.
		Reduction-fired wares – clay wall too thin to withstand extra compressive load of glaze in this type of firing.	Increase the thickness of the clay wall slightly – apply thinner coat of glaze. Test first in an oxidized firing to check if the problem is arising in the reduction firing.

PATCHY COLOUR/ COLOUR VARIATIONS **Applies to:** Coloured glazes, mainly.	Inconsistent colour coverage. See Uneven glaze, page 22.	Zircon opacified coloured glaze – segregating into light and dark areas.	Increase zircon content in glaze (also increase stain content). Or use a refractory stain and replace some of the zircon with tin oxide.
		Vapour contamination from oxides and other colourants in the same glaze firing.	Where possible, fire one type of glaze at a time. Pack the kiln less tightly to allow greater movement of air around wares in electric kilns.
		Trapped bubbles in glaze.	Raise biscuit firing temperature slightly. Check glaze content has not changed (new source of an ingredient). Slow down firing and make sure the kiln is firing to optimum temperature for glaze. See Firing chart on page 117.
GRITTY GLAZE SURFACE – KNOWN AS BITTINESS **Applies to:** Most commonly in alkaline glazes.	Imperfections in the fired surface that feel rough to the touch.	Improperly sieved glaze.	Re-sieve through a finer mesh.
		Contamination of glaze after mixing.	Re-sieve to remove contaminant.
		Crystal formation in slop glaze that has been unused for some time.	Store glaze in the coolest place possible – heat encourages crystal formation. Sieving out the crystals will not affect the nature of the glaze.
BLISTERING **Applies to:** All glazes.	Craters, bubbles and pinholes in the fired glaze.	Over-firing.	Reduce the firing temperature and length of firing.
		Rapid firing – rapid cooling.	Slow down temperature rise as glaze matures – soak glaze. Slow down the cooling rate over 100°C (212°F) from top temperature (fire down).
		Some wares placed too close to kiln elements.	Observe where the problem arose in the kiln – reposition wares in subsequent firings
		Flame flashing in gas or oil-fired kilns.	Position wares away from direct contact with flame.
		Glaze ingredients.	Try replacing feldspar or nepheline syenite in part with borax frit – test! Reduce whiting content – replace with wollastonite (calcium silicate).
		Colouring oxides, especially manganese.	Fire slowly, lengthen soak and cool slowly.
BLOATING **Applies to:** Higher-firing clays firing to vitrification – stonewares and porcelains.	Bulges appearing as swollen bubbles or small blisters that appear to be trapped in the clay body after glaze firing.	Over-firing.	Reduce maturing temperature – test in small increments to find optimum top temperature.
		Rapid firing.	Slow down the firing ramp (see Kilns and firing, page 117).
		Clay body.	Decrease volatile material content of clay or change clay.

PATCHES OF CLAY SHOWING THROUGH THE GLAZE – KNOWN AS CRAWLING Applies to: All glazes.	Glaze appears to have separated into lumps and beads on the surface of wares.	Dusty or greasy areas on biscuit ware repelling glaze.	Ensure surfaces are dust-free – avoid excessive handling before glazing. Re-biscuit fire if unsure.
		Glaze ingredients – zinc colemenite applied too thickly.	Reduce thickness of glaze – apply in two thin coats rather than one. Replace ingredients in part with calcium borate frit, and fire more slowly.
		Underglaze colours.	Mix colours with a little glaze before application, or add 1–3% glaze binder. **Try also:** firing the colour on to 600°C (1112°F) before applying glaze.
		Raw glazed wares – too-rapid firing.	Spray glazes where possible. Slow firing rate, especially over the first 600°C (1112°F) – it should be slower than for biscuit firing (see page 117). Keep the kiln well ventilated.
		Soluble salts in the clay body causing deposits – may be present in water supply also having the same effect.	Add barium carbonate to the clay body. Add a little vinegar to water used when throwing/making, etc.
		Drying shrinkage of glaze too high.	Replace some of the clay content of the glaze with calcined clay – Replace ball clay with china clay or calcined china clay (molochite).
MILKY-LOOKING TRANS-PARENT GLAZE Applies to: Transparent glazes.	Fired glaze is opaque in places and sometimes appears purplish in colour or clouded by tiny little bubbles.	Glaze applied too thickly.	Scrape away and smooth back glaze after dipping especially in areas like the bottoms of bowls, mugs, etc. Thin down glaze.
		Under-firing.	Check firing temperature for clay and glaze (see Firing chart, page 117). Fire the glaze a little higher or soak glaze at top temperature for 10 minutes or so.
ORANGE PEEL OR DIMPLED GLAZE (NOT TO BE CONFUSED WITH SALT GLAZE) Applies to: All glazes.	The glazed surface is dimpled, resembling orange peel.	Biscuit temperature too low.	Fire biscuit to higher temperature (see Firing chart, page 117).
		Glaze application – common in sprayed glazes.	Spray items from further away or reduce the pressure a little.
		Fast firing.	Slow down firing cycle – or lengthen the soak period.
		Under-firing or over-firing.	Modify firing rates accordingly.
		Glaze ingredients	Replace whiting with wollastonite, or dolomite with a mixture of wollastonite and talc or magnesium carbonate. Reduce alumina or clay content of glaze.

CRAZING Applies to: All glazes.	The fired glaze appears full of cracked lines that can present as large streaks or a fine network.	Under-firing.	Fire the clay body to at least its minimum temperature in order for glaze to fit, but preferably somewhere in the middle of its firing range.
		Firing too quickly.	See Firing chart, page 117.
		Low expansion clay bodies – stonewares, raku bodies and porcelain fired at low temperatures.	Unless crazing is used for effect – modify the clay body by adding flint or cristobolite – test in small additions until required result is achieved.
		Thermal expansion of glaze too high.	Add quartz or flint to the glaze plus a small amount of borax frit or lead bisilicate in earthenware glazes. Add dolomite or whiting in stoneware glazes. **Try also:** Adding 5% zircon. Replace soda, alumina, potash with lead oxide, zirconia, magnesia, boric or zinc oxide. Use lithium-based frit in alkaline glaze if crazing is undesirable.
		Opening the kiln too soon – heat shock.	Open kilns at room temperature only – never above 100°C (212°F).
		Metal oxides in glaze.	Fire higher, soak for longer or add quartz or flint to the glaze.
		Mismatched slip and clay body.	Where possible mix slip from the same clay body (most useful with white-firing clays). If not possible, an equal amount of ball clay, china clay and flint will suit most earthenware bodies.
		Glaze too thick.	Thin glaze down – the thinner the coat the less likelihood of crazing.
PINHOLING Applies to: All glazes.	Tiny marks, the size of pinholes, that look like burst bubbles.	Biscuit firing too low.	Increase biscuit temperature – test in small increments.
		Rapid firing.	Slow down the firing rate – increase soak to a half hour – slow down cooling for first 100°C (212°F).
		Reduced glaze pick up/covering – common on cast and thin walled wares.	Use a heavier glaze mix.
		Glaze materials.	Soften glaze to make flow more easily. For earthenware, add lead bisilicate or standard borax frit; for stoneware, add colemenite, nepheline syenite or feldspar.
		Contamination – dust, etc.	Clean all surfaces before glazing – refire if necessary. Re-sieve glaze to remove possible contaminants.
PEELING (ALSO KNOWN AS SHIVERING) Applies to: All glazes.	Looks like crazing but the edges of the cracks feel sharp. Particularly obvious at rims and edges where the glaze shears away.	Compressive forces in the glaze that prevent bonding with the clay body.	Increase the coefficient of expansion of the glaze: Stoneware – equal parts (2:1) frit and china clay; Earthenware – 5 parts frit to 1 part china clay. Apply glaze more thinly. Decrease the coefficient expansion of the clay body: Reduce flint – partly replace with quartz. Reduce iron and lime content. Change grog content – replace sand with molochite or finely ground fire brick. Reduce maximum firing temperature.
		Deposits on the clay surface from soluble salts.	See also Scumming, page 42.
		Poorly matched slip/engobe to clay body.	See also Flaking on greenware and biscuit ware, page 98.

PROBLEM	DESCRIPTION	CAUSES	FIX BY
GLAZE RUN OFF RESULTING IN POTS STICKING TO KILN SHELF **Applies to:** All glazes.	Glaze melts so much in firing it runs off the surface and pools at the base sticking the form to the kiln shelf.	Incorrect glaze constituents for firing temperature.	Replace some of the flint or quartz in the glaze for china clay.
		Over-firing.	Try firing at a slightly lower temperature 10–20°C (50–60°F).
		Colouring oxide acting as a flux.	Add half the weight of oxide in china clay to the glaze. Reduce firing temperature slightly – see above. **Try also:** Bat-washing kiln shelves or using placing sand on kiln shelves.
SPECKING **Applies to:** All glazes.	Glaze looks rough and feels gritty to the touch.	Contamination from: Machinery used in making, sieves, water supply, containers.	Put glaze through sufficiently fine sieve – with no defects in the lawn – to remove most contaminants.
		Colouring agents.	Use gum or SCMC binder to fix colour before glazing or fire colour on before glazing.
		Firing – kiln brick – placing sand, etc.	Clean kiln between firings. Replace sand on kiln shelf for bat wash. See also Specking in the clay body, page 16.
		Burners used in gas kilns.	Use a filter on the burner.
COLOUR TRANSFER **Applies to:** White and copper oxide glazes in same firing.	Pots covered in white glaze look green when fired.	Copper contamination – very volatile oxide.	Fire white wares separate from wares with copper oxide in the glaze – if not completely at least on separate shelves.
CHROME GREEN GLAZE FIRING PINK **Applies to:** Glazes using chrome as a colourant.	Glaze intended to be green comes out of the kiln pink.	Tin oxide used as an opacifier in the glaze mix.	Use zirconium instead of tin, or choose a different green colourant.

SURFACE DECORATION – GENERAL FAULTS

PROBLEM	DESCRIPTION	CAUSES	FIX BY
COLOURING PIGMENTS			
COLOUR APPLICATION **Applies to:** Underglaze colours and oxides onto biscuit ware or unfired glaze surfaces.	Difficulty in application of underglaze and overglaze colours and oxides.	Brush dragging on porous biscuit surface.	Dip wares into water prior to colour application to reduce porosity, mix the colour with oil medium, or apply the colour onto clayware – beyond leather hard but not completely dry. **Try also:** mix 2–5% sodium carboxymethyl cellulose into the colour.
		Brush dragging over glaze surface in majolica decoration.	Make the glaze surface harder by adding 0.5–2% gum or glaze binder. **Try also:** Mixing some of the glaze with the colour before application.
		Differential in firing temperatures of various colours.	Fire colours onto biscuit in stages – highest-temperature colours first then lower temperatures. Apply large areas of colour with a fine sponge in a stippling action.

MILKY-LOOKING	Glaze appears cloudy or milky over colour-decorated areas.	Devitrification or crystallization of glaze.	Change from borax to fritted lead-based glaze. Fire biscuit to the same temperature as the glaze. Do not soak the glaze. Cool from top temperature as quickly as possible down to the liquidus point. Add up to 5% alumina or china clay to the glaze to make more viscous.
BLACKENING **Applies to:** Colours used in majolica technique.	Areas of colour appear blackened especially at edges or the end of brush strokes.	Poor fusion of colour and glaze.	Mix some of the glaze with the colour before application. Or add 10–50% of an alternative flux like lead bisilicate or borax – some experimentation required. Be aware of metal release issues if using copper oxide with lead-based glazes.
		Inappropriate reduction atmosphere in kiln.	Ensure adequate space between wares in the kiln and that the ventilation is sufficient for the type of firing.
MATT OVERGLAZE **Applies to:** Overglaze colours that should fire shiny.	Overglaze colours look matt instead of shiny when fired.	Over-firing or under-firing.	Check kiln programmer is working correctly.
		Volatile agents in the kiln atmosphere.	Leave bungs out when firing to allow adequate ventilation.
		Cooling phase too slow.	Speed up cooling from top temperature by removing the vent bung for 10–20 minutes after the firing is complete. Replace to allow cooling at normal rate thereafter.
		Colour contamination with crystallizing agents.	Avoid use with whiting, zinc oxide, wollastonite or dolomite.
		Mixing overglaze with underglaze colour.	Ensure all dry materials are properly marked to avoid mix-ups.
GLAZE CRAWL **Applies to:** Glaze applied over underglaze colours.	Glaze crawls over colour decoration leaving areas unglazed.	Colours acting as a resist – not providing an adequately wetted surface for glaze to adhere.	Add some glaze or flux to the colouring pigment.
		Gas produced by decomposition of the colour or medium used to apply it.	Apply colour more thinly. Reduce the amount of medium used. Fire more slowly up to 500°C (932°F).
	Colour decoration runs and blurs especially where cobalt or nickel have been used on a fluid glaze.	Glaze too fluid.	Add 5–10% china clay or alumina to the glaze to increase viscosity.
		Glaze too thick.	Thin the glaze and keep coverage as thin as possible.
		Firing temperature too high.	Lower the firing temperature a little. Dispense with the soaking phase at the top end of firing.
BUBBLY OR FRIZZLED OVERGLAZE COLOURS **Applies to:** Colours applied over glaze.	Overglaze decoration feels rough or has tiny bubbles over the surface.	Gases escaping or erupting during the burning of organic material in the medium.	Reduce the amount of medium used, or try another medium with less organic content.
		Rapid firing.	Fire more slowly.
		Poor kiln ventilation.	Leave bungs out until a later stage when firing.

SPIT OUT **Applies to:** Overglaze colours, decal and lustre decoration on earthenware.	The glazed surface is roughened with a covering of tiny broken blisters.	Water vapour trapped in glazed wares has penetrated the porous clay body.	Reduce overglaze firing temperature by 5–10°C (10–20°F). Biscuit fire higher.
COLOUR CHANGES IN	Changes in colour response from previous firings.	New source of colours.	Test new colours before use – unglazed and glazed – if colour only changes after glazing the problem lies with the glaze.
		New/different glaze.	Use low solubility lead glazes for best colour response.
		Glaze too thick.	Water glaze down slightly, and apply more thinly.
		Colour application too thin and burning away in firing.	Apply colours in an even thickness.
		High firing – colour burnout.	Modify glaze firing temperature to accommodate reds, pinks and some yellows, which fire out at higher temperatures.
COLOUR CHANGES IN OVERGLAZE DECORATION **Applies to:** Any surface decorated by this method.	Most commonly colours appear blackened or to have disappeared in firing. Liquid gold fires purple.	Over-firing.	Check kiln is firing properly. Fire in the range of 700–750°C (1292–1382°F).
		Under-firing.	Re-fire in the same range as above.
		Selenium reds – poor application.	Apply a good, even coat, and ensure a good oxidation atmosphere in the kiln when firing.
		Reaction with liquid gold lustre.	Avoid firing lead antimonate (Naples yellow) with liquid gold.
		Application too thin.	Apply in two thin coats.
BADLY FIRED DECAL HOLES **Applies to:** Any surface decorated by this method.	Decals have holes with raised edges after firing.	Water trapped underneath the decal during application.	Use a cloth or squeegee to smooth the decal onto the surface and wipe away all underlying water.
LUSTRE COLOUR NOT FIRING TRUE **Applies to:** Gold especially but also other colours.	Colours fire to a pinkish/purple hue.	Contamination from colour to colour.	Always use a separate brush for each colour.
		Over-firing – colour starts to burn out.	Fire lustres at 750°C (1380°F) for best results.
	Lustres rub off after firing.	Under-firing or poor glaze.	Replace the glaze with one that melts at the correct temperature for lustre decoration.
PORCELAIN AND BONE CHINA BLACK SPOT **Applies to:** Porcelain and bone china only.	Black spots appearing on porcelain or bone china after the decoration firing.	The burning of organic material present in the medium used for colour application.	Change to water-based medium. Leave the bungs out of the kiln until 650°C (1202°F) to improve ventilation. Fire more slowly. Apply colour decoration in two or more firings. Change source of porcelain or bone china.

FIRING – SPECIFIC FAULTS

PROBLEM	DESCRIPTION	CAUSES	FIX BY
SMOKE FIRING			
BAD ADHESION OF SLIP RESIST **Applies to:** Especially to burnished surfaces, but also non-burnished surfaces.	Slip peels away from the clay surface as it dries.	Biscuit too high – surface not porous enough.	Biscuit fire between 900–1000°C(1652–1832°F).
		Clay wall too thin – making the surface lack porosity.	Build the forms with a thicker wall section. Make the resist slip from the same clay as the form with addition of gum arabic – sieve through 200s mesh.
		Terra sigillata – surface appears vitrified making adhesion difficult.	Reduce biscuit temperature a little. Make a slip for burnishing from the clay body with grogs sieved out as an alternative to terra sigillata.
INABILITY TO REMOVE SLIP AFTER FIRING **Applies to:** Low-fired clay surfaces.	Slip sticks solidly to the surface after smoke firing when it should fall away like eggshell.	Biscuit firing too low.	Biscuit fire in the range suggested above for best results.
		Over-firing in smoke bin – temperature too high causing fusion of slip and clay body.	Try smoking with combustible materials like newspaper or straw as an alternative to sawdust. Use wood shavings instead of fine sawdust.
		Poor burnishing making the surface too porous – allowing the slip and clay to bond in firing.	Improve burnishing to compact the clay surface more – burnish at several stages for best results. **Try also:** Soak the form in water for a few minutes after firing to soften the slip before removing with a plastic rib.
TANNIN MARKS **Applies to:** Unresisted surfaces in smoke firing.	Brown stains on the surface of the form.	Resins from sawdust or shavings dripping from the lid of the smoke bin.	Change to hard wood shavings if possible; pine shavings are the worst. Change to another combustible – paper or straw for example. Leave the lid off the bin – cover with fine-mesh chicken wire instead. Re-biscuit fire the form if all else fails.
CRACKS **Applies to:** Specific to this type of firing.	Dramatic cracks often splitting forms in half or shattering completely.	Thermal shock.	Leave forms to cool in the smoking bin rather than lifting into a cooler atmosphere.
		Poor construction.	Ensure walls are of even thickness throughout the form.
		Bad design – some forms are ill-suited to smoke firing.	Avoid slab-built forms – ensure closed pinch forms have a hole pierced in them. Pay extra attention to joins.
		Wrong clay.	Change to clay with good thermal shock properties – grogged varieties work best. Try adding some grog to your clay. See Clay types: composition and nature, page 42.

FIRING – SPECIFIC FAULTS

PROBLEM	DESCRIPTION	CAUSES	FIX BY
RAKU FIRING			
INABILITY TO REMOVE GLAZE **Applies to** Naked or resist raku.	Glaze that should shell away from the body easily sticks to the form.	Resist slip layer insufficiently thick – glaze sticking to body.	Pour or dip the resist slip for best and even coverage. Aim for a covering of about 3 mm (⅛ in).
		Firing temperature too high.	Lower the temperature a little – glaze barely needs to melt for this technique.
INABILITY TO REMOVE SLIP POST-FIRING **Applies to:** Naked or resist raku.	Glaze shells away, but the underlying slip is difficult to remove from the surface.	High firing causing slip to bond with the clay body.	Reduce firing temperature a little. Add 5–10% aluminium hydroxide to the slip to prevent adhesion. Wearing a good dust mask, use a nylon scourer to remove slip – be careful not to scratch the burnished surface.
PINHOLE SMOKE MARKS ON THE SURFACE **Applies to:** Naked or resist raku.	Once cleaned, the surface of the form is covered with tiny black smoke marks.	Air bubbles trapped in the resist slip.	Allow slip to stand for a while after mixing – mix carefully to avoid incorporating air.
		Air bubbles in glaze.	Allow glaze to stand for a while after mixing – mix carefully to avoid incorporating air. Try applying glaze by a different method.
		Contaminants in slip or glaze.	Keep buckets covered when not in use – sieve again if in doubt.
		Dust on the surface of the form before slip/glazing.	Wipe surfaces with a barely damp cloth before applying slip.
		Reaction with specking agents in the clay body.	Cover the form with a slip made from the same body with grog sieved out prior to burnishing. Burnish to a higher degree to compact the clay. Change clay!
		Removing the pot from the kiln too soon.	Remove the pots just after the glaze has melted and bubbles have smoothed over. Use the effect as a feature.
INABILITY TO APPLY GLAZE **Applies to:** Naked or resist raku.	Difficulty applying glaze over resist slip.	Both slip and glaze are white, making it difficult to see which is which.	Stain the slip with a brightly coloured food dye.
		Brush dragging over the underlying slip.	Pour, dip or spray the glaze over the base slip. Or make the glaze a little thinner – load onto a large mop brush and work on a banding wheel – apply two coats to be sure.

INABILITY TO APPLY DECORATIVE RESISTS OVER SLIP RESIST **Applies to:** Naked or resist raku.	Wax or latex resist peels away when applied over resist slip. *Note this is a difficult technique to master and takes practice.	Powdery slip surface.	Avoid handling the form as much as possible once the slip is applied. Avoid touching the wax or latex once applied. Try decorating the biscuit surface first then applying slip and glaze over the top. Latex can be removed carefully before firing; wax will burn away.
		Brush adhering to slip surface.	Use wax emulsion, watered down slightly to make more fluid. Load brush and work quickly – don't allow it to linger on the surface
UNEVEN SMOKING **Applies to:** Naked or resist raku.	The fired form is black in some areas – pale in others.	The way the form is placed in the smoking bin – that is where one side of the form contacts the combustible material more than the rest of the form.	Try to stand the form upright inside the bin – on a thin layer of wood shavings – sprinkle shavings over the top to cover evenly then seal down the lid. Use smaller bins – reduce forms individually.
		Too long in the smoking bin.	Remove the forms a little sooner – allow to cool in another container without combustible content.
		Uneven application of resist slip or glaze.	Dip, pour or spray slip/glaze for best and even application.
EXPLOSIONS **Applies to:** Traditional or resist raku.	Wares explode in the kiln when being lifted from the kiln, or during post-firing treatments.	In the kiln, insufficient drying before firing.	Allow wares to dry completely before firing. Glaze a day in advance of firing – place the forms in a warm spot to dry.
		Thermal shock – cold wares going into a hot kiln.	Stand wares on top of the kiln as it heats up to warm them through.
		Wrong clay.	Choose clay with good thermal shock properties – ask your supplier for advice. Generally, grogged clay works best.
		Lifting out of the kiln (thermal shock) due to cold atmospheric temperature or wind.	Fire in a sheltered spot if possible – under a fire-proof canopy. Avoid firing on days of extreme temperature – hot is better than cold!
		Quenching wares in water to cool rapidly or seal a surface effect.	Don't do it! Allow the work to cool naturally in the reduction bin or move items to another bin without combustibles.
PINHOLING, CRATERING **Applies to:** Traditional raku.	The glaze appears to have myriad tiny burst bubbles.	The causes can be any of those mentioned in Glaze: Faults in fired surfaces: pinholing on page 26, but generally result from poor judgement of glaze melt in raku firing.	Fire until the glaze looks shiny and even and all bubbles have burst and settled. Turn off the heat source – allow the glaze to settle for a moment or two before lifting out of the kiln.

UNEVEN FIRING **Applies to:** Mostly traditional raku.	The surface of the form is cratered with bubbles on one side only.	Partial over-firing due to wares being directly in the line of the gas flame.	Pack the kiln to avoid placing forms in the path of the flame – it may mean firing fewer pieces.
GLAZE FALL OFF WHEN PLACING IN RAKU KILN **Applies to:** Mostly traditional, but occasionally resist raku.	Bits of glaze flake from the surface of the form as it is placed in the kiln.	The glaze has not dried out completely.	Dry pots on top of the kiln as it heats up prior to firing. Glaze a day in advance to allow thorough drying.

FIRING – GENERAL FAULTS

PROBLEM	DESCRIPTION	CAUSES	FIX BY
INSIDE THE KILN			
WARES ADHERING TO KILN SHELF **Applies to:** Mostly glazed wares, can affect unglazed items in some cases.	Wares are fixed to the kiln shelf after firing.	Glaze melt/run off.	See Glaze: Faults in fired surfaces: glaze run off on page 27.
		Colouring oxides fluxing the glaze.	Add half colouring oxide in china clay to the glaze to counteract. Apply glaze at a higher point on the form to allow the glaze more room to flow down. Reduce firing temperature a little.
		Forgetting to remove glaze from foot rings and bases of pots.	Wax bases and foot rings before applying glaze. Wipe over before firing to ensure no small drops of glaze are still attached. Or simply wipe glaze away around bases using a damp sponge after application.
		Firing at high temperatures – foot rings fuse to kiln shelf even though there is no glaze contact.	Use either bat wash on kiln shelves or a very fine layer of placing sand or alumina – make sure the sand or alumina does not come into contact with glaze.
UNEVEN FIRING **Applies to:** Wares fired in electric kilns mainly, but can apply to gas kilns.		Element failure.	Check that all elements are working correctly – have the kiln serviced regularly.
		Faulty programmer.	Have the kiln serviced regularly. Testing the firing with pyrometric cones will determine if it is firing correctly.
		Overloaded kiln.	Allow a little more space between items (see Kiln housekeeping, page 122).
		Wares packed too close to the heat source.	Avoid placing items too close to elements in electric kilns or flames in gas and raku kilns (see Kiln housekeeping, page 122).

CHAPTER 2

CLAYS

AS A MAKER YOU WILL ENCOUNTER FAR FEWER PROBLEMS
IF YOU BEGIN WITH A SOLID UNDERSTANDING OF CLAY:
WHAT IT IS, WHERE IT COMES FROM AND HOW IT BEHAVES
AT VARIOUS STAGES. FROM ITS SOURCE TO PREPARATION
AND THEN ON TO BUILDING AND FIRING, THIS CHAPTER
WORKS THROUGH ALL THE INFORMATION YOU WILL NEED
FOR BEST PRACTICE. THIS ADVICE WILL HELP YOU TO AVOID
PROBLEMS BEFORE THEY ARISE.

The nature of clays

Few of us want to read through reams of technical stuff to solve our potting problems, especially when time is pressing, but many problems arise out of a basic lack of understanding of what clay can and can't do. To really get to the root of certain problems, it helps to know what clay is made from, how raw deposits are affected by geological influences and how commercial manufacturers process the raw materials to make the products that we buy bagged and ready for use.

What is clay?

In the most simple terms, clay is a naturally occurring material that is found almost everywhere in the world. It is an incredibly malleable substance, made from fine-grained rock, and has the important quality of plasticity, which enables it to be formed and retain a shape. It can be seen as seams running through the sides of riverbeds or in cliff faces and is often exposed in the excavation of roads, especially when cutting through hillsides. It is recognizable as a smooth and compact material sandwiched between coarser layers of gravel, sand or earth and it can even be found in domestic gardens.

Most clay bodies are composed from the minerals alumina and silica, with small amounts of other minerals, which act as fluxes. These two components are chemically transformed when heated and fuse or melt together in the firing process, becoming hard and tough when cooled.

PRIMARY OR RESIDUAL CLAYS

Clays that remain at their original site of decomposition are known as primary or residual clays and are characterized by their refractoriness (they do not melt much below 1750°C/3182°F).

High proportions of rocks in the earth's crust contain the mineral feldspar and are referred to as being feldspathic. A common example is granite.

When granite is altered by hydrothermal action, it produces the mineral kaolinite, which, in large accumulations, makes up deposits of kaolin or china clay, the material from which many clays are manufactured, especially porcelains. Very pure deposits of china clay are found in Devon and Cornwall in the UK and in North Carolina in the US, but, unlike those mined in China, they are nonplastic and are therefore not suitable for working in their natural state; they have to be mixed with other clay materials to make a working body.

SECONDARY OR SEDIMENTARY CLAYS

When primary clays are moved from their original site by the action of water in streams and rivers or by glaciers and deposited in other sites in sedimentary layers, they are referred to as secondary clays. Movement and weathering grinds the clay particles to a very fine state: they become laminatory (i.e. they are laid down in planes parallel to one another) in structure, making some, especially certain ball clays, very plastic.

▼ These samples of clays from around the world show the diverse colour range of clays in their raw state.

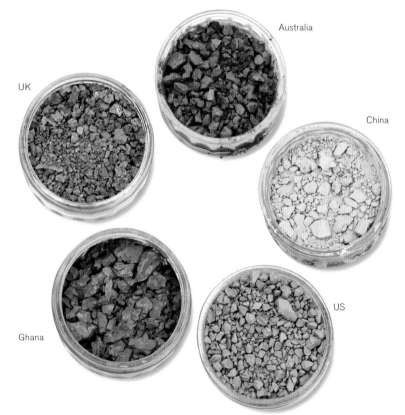

Australia

UK

China

Ghana

US

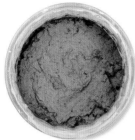

▼ Ball clay (left) and fireclay (right), two materials widely used in the production of clay bodies.

In the course of being transported, the clays can pick up many impurities that affect colour and shrinkage when fired. They can be anything from white to dark brown, depending on the type and quantity of impurities. Uncontaminated sedimentary clays are known as ball clays. In their raw state they range in colour from black to blue because of the presence of decomposed vegetable matter; this burns away in the course of firing to reveal a clay that is white, off-white or buff.

Clay that is transported from its original site by glaciers is known as boulder clay. Without the washing effect of flowing water, the clay is trapped in the ice along with rocks, stones, pebbles and other impurities; when it is finally deposited, it still contains these materials.

Ball clay is vitrifiable; for this reason, along with its other qualities of plasticity and purity, it is commonly used in the production of stoneware and earthenware bodies.

Other sedimentary clays collect different mineral and organic materials during transportation. Red clays contain large amounts of iron oxide, a very common mineral that gives the characteristic colour. This type of clay is highly plastic, with a low melting point, and is traditionally used for making domestic wares, garden pots (terracotta) and bricks.

Fireclay is a highly refractory (high-firing) sedimentary clay commonly used to make bricks. It can be very coarse in structure and is added to stoneware bodies to produce a more open texture and speckling under reduction firing. These clays can fire from light to warm buff colours, but are darker under reduction. Fireclay is dried and/or calcined, then crushed, ground and screened before it is blended with other materials to make a working body. The process of calcining involves firing the clay to a very high temperature to eliminate moisture and organic material; it causes a chemical reaction

CONVERSION OF FELDSPAR TO CLAY

PROCESS OF BREAKDOWN	CHEMICAL COMPOSITION
KAOLINIZATION	
Feldspar	Alumina, silica, alkalis
↓	
Water action	
↓	
Kaolin	Alumina, silica, water + a few impurities
↓	
Decomposition	
↓	
Primary or residual clay	Alumina, silica, water + a few impurities
↓	
Clay is transported by water or glacier	
↓	
Sedimentary clay	Alumina, silica, water + many more impurities
	Clay now has smaller particle size
	Laminatory in structure

CONVERSION OF FELDSPAR TO CHINA CLAY

PROCESS OF BREAKDOWN	CHEMICAL COMPOSITION
Feldspar	Alumina, silica, alkalis
↓	
Hydrothermal action	
↓	
Kaolinite	Alumina, silica, water
↓	
Decomposition	
↓	
China clay	Alumina, silica, water

between the alumina and silica, rendering a harder, denser material that is more easily crushed to produce various grades of fireclay grog.

Within this broad overview of clay classifications, there is a wide variety of clays, each laid down by geological influences specific to its location. Weathering conditions, along with organic and other impurities, will all have had an effect on the texture, colour and workability of these clays to give the potter choices for experimentation and development.

Clay bodies – what are they?

Few clays can be used directly from the ground; other additives have to be introduced to give particular attributes – for example, to aid plasticity, lower or raise firing temperature or change colour.

When clays and other materials are combined in this way, the resulting product is referred to as a clay body. Most commercially available clays are prepared by blending different raw materials. Highly plastic ball clay forms the basis of most prepared bodies (along with other ingredients such as bentonite) to provide handling strength. In addition, other minerals such as feldspar, alumina or silica, or nonplastic materials such as china clay, china stone or whiting can be included to give a body the characteristics required by the potter.

In general, the greater the amount of clay in a clay body the greater the green strength (unfired strength) – but also, the greater the wet-to-dry shrinkage.

Ball clays are more plastic than fireclays (with some exceptions) and very much more so than china clays, so replacing the first with the latter will greatly reduce green strength.

The addition of grog reduces green strength but also reduces shrinkage and improves thermal resistance, making a body less likely to crack in firing.

Clay bodies are generally classified in three main types: earthenware, stoneware and porcelain. Within each category there are numerous variations to choose from.

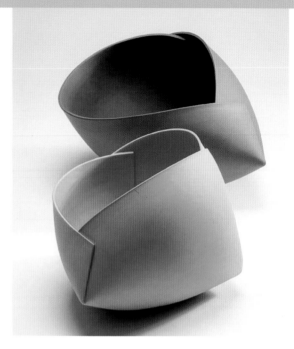

▲ ANN VAN HOEY
These finely made slab forms have been cut and folded like origami while being supported in plaster moulds during construction and drying.

Clay bodies, produced by mixing various materials for specific qualities including colour and firing ability.

▶ A very dark grey stoneware clay with flecks of iron dispersed throughout.

▶ The high iron content gives red stoneware clay its colour.

▶ Porcelain is a very white clay.

▶ A standard, buff-coloured stoneware clay.

▶ White earthenware is grey before it is fired.

▶ Red earthenware.

EARTHENWARE CLAYS

Earthenware clays are generally fired within the range of 1050–1150°C (1922–2102°F). However, it should be noted that there are some broad-spectrum clays available that are classed as earthenware or stoneware because they will fire up to stoneware temperatures, making them very versatile bodies.

Earthenware is characterized by its porosity when fired and can be any colour from the familiar terracotta red through white to buff.

White-burning earthenware bodies have low green strength because they are made up from other materials – china clay and ball clay, plus up to 50 per cent non-clay ingredients such as feldspar, Cornish stone or flint. Talc is another constituent that is widely added to low-firing, white-burning bodies; to prevent moisture expansion, it is added in large amounts to tile bodies. The advantage of these bodies is their low wet-to-dry shrinkage.

Red earthenware clays are generally made up from blended red marls. They may include some ball clay or fireclay but otherwise no 'filler', making their green strength good but wet-to-dry shrinkage high. Sand or grog can be added to compensate for this; to counteract the problem in redware casting slips, 20 per cent fine quartz sand is included as a filler.

STONEWARE CLAYS

Stoneware clays generally fire within the range of 1200–1300°C (2192–2372°F) and are characterized by the fact that they become vitreous when fired.

They are made from fireclays or ball clays, or combinations of both with little or no filler, although grog or sand is often added to reduce high shrinkage rates in bodies like these that are made purely from clay. This unfortunately has the effect of reducing the green strength of stoneware bodies.

In their raw state, most stoneware clay bodies are various shades of grey in colour. Firing from grey to warm buff or white, the final colour is also affected by the type of firing the wares have gone through – oxidized or reduction.

▼ GAIL NICHOLS
This vessel showcases soda vapour glazing. The work is gas-fired to Orton cone 11 and the soda is introduced at cone 9–10.

PORCELAIN BODIES

Porcelain bodies fire in the range of 1220–1350°C (2228–2462°F) and are characterized by being white, vitreous and opaque or translucent when fired. Known for being difficult to handle because of their critical moisture range, porcelains can quickly move from being too soft to too dry.

Generally made up from china clay, feldspar and quartz, porcelains do not contain ball clays because they destroy translucency. bentonite or organic plasticizers can be added to improve workability (especially for throwing bodies), but they have very low green strength and wet-to-dry shrinkage.

Other white-firing bodies include bone china – a type of soft-paste porcelain. It is a vitreous body known for its whiteness and translucency and used extensively in the tableware industry. It is generally made up from about 50 per cent calcined bone ash with china stone and china clay. It is a particularly 'unplastic' body, rarely worked by hand and most commonly slip cast. It differs greatly from other bodies in that it has a short firing range: as soon as it reaches its eutectic temperature (the lowest melting point of two or more constituents), the body becomes chemically fluid really quickly, which can cause the form to deform – so warpage is very common and there is a high loss rate.

Standard firing temperatures also differ in that biscuit is fired to 1250°C (2282°F) with a 1½-hour soak, taking the body to vitrification, but glazed only to 1080°C (1976°F).

▲ JO DAVIES
These irregular forms have a light-hearted sensuality that lacks the formal rigidity of many geometric shapes. They are wheel-thrown in porcelain, modified while wet and finished with an opaque crackle glaze.

Clay processing

Slip housing is the industrial process used to make clays that we buy ready for use. The process is the best method for making highly refined white bodies and removes about half of any soluble salts in the body:

1 Constituent dry materials are either put into a blunger or a blending ark with water to reduce to slip.

2 The slip is filtered (whiteware bodies are also passed over electromagnets to remove iron and other impurities).

3 The purified body is stored in large agitators or arks.

4 From here the slip is pumped to filter presses, where it is dewatered to make 'filter cake clay'.

5 The filter cake is put through a pug mill.

Pan milling is a less labour-intensive production method that produces better plastic clay and is therefore used where a less refined body is required. Dry ingredients are mixed with slip and/or water in a pan mill or dough mixer. This method is more open to contamination than slip housing, but allows for greater control of water content and grog.

Powdered clay bodies are generally made from dried filter cake that has been crushed in a pan mill or other type of mill.

Casting slips are made either from filter cake, dry ingredients or plastic clay.

Special bodies – paper clay, fibre clay – are made from any of the clay types with the addition of 5–50 per cent paper, nylon fibre, etc. They are unique in that completely dry clay sections can be joined to wet with no cracking or warpage problems, making it ideal for sculptural forms.

AGEING CLAY

After production, clay is generally stored for six to 10 weeks to improve plasticity and workability. This is more important for pan-milled clays because they do not go through the lengthy slaking process of slip-housed varieties, but all clays improve with ageing if kept in the right conditions at even temperatures, away from extreme sources of heat or cold. This also applies to reclaimed clay.

Typical slip-housing layout

▼ The chart shows a typical sequence in the slip-housing process for production of stoneware and whiteware clay bodies.

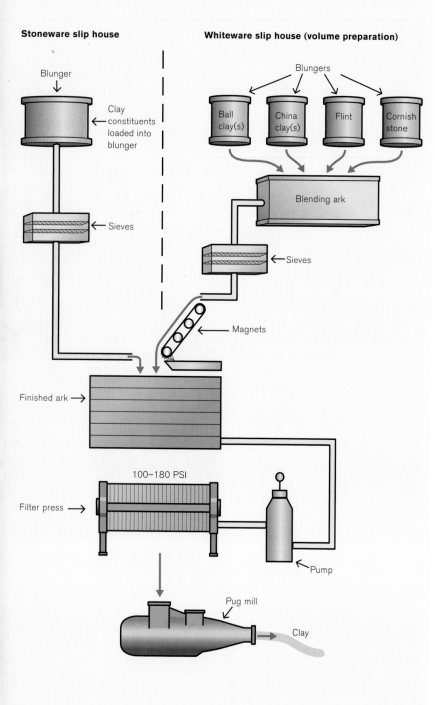

Stoneware slip house

Blunger

Clay constituents loaded into blunger

Sieves

Finished ark

100–180 PSI

Filter press

Pug mill

Whiteware slip house (volume preparation)

Blungers

Ball clay(s)

China clay(s)

Flint

Cornish stone

Blending ark

Sieves

Magnets

Pump

Clay

BEST PRACTICE

Clay particle orientation

Sounds boring and too technical? Think again! Understanding where clay comes from is important, but it is also vital to be aware of what is happening within the structure of a clay body as it is processed and then formed, because some very specific problems relate to the incorrect orientation of clay particles.

What is a clay particle?

We have already established that plasticity is a valuable characteristic of sedimentary clay and that it is brought about by the geological influences of movement, which break down the particles to smaller and smaller sizes the further the clay travels from its original site.

The actual particles can be most likened in shape to small plates. When floated in water and allowed to settle gently, the plates align in planes parallel to one another, with the maximum surface areas all lying in the same direction.

The particles in residual clays are much coarser because they lack the grinding action of movement and consequently have a random distribution.

In the course of processing, the plate-like clay

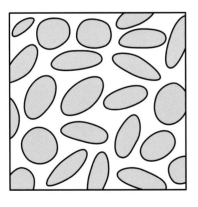

◄ Particle distribution in residual clays is random, particles are coarse and irregular in shape, lying at many different angles.

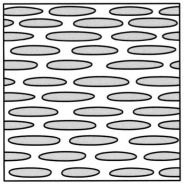

◄ Sedimentary clays show finer-grained particles lying in planes, parallel to one another.

particles angle themselves at 90° to the pressure being applied. When the clay is pugged, therefore, the pressure applied as it is forced through the extrusion process causes the plates to align parallel to one another within the surface layers, but in a more random arrangement at the core. Because there is less shrinkage in clay that has fewer gaps between particles (the outer or surface layers of the pugged clay) and greater shrinkage within the randomly orientated clay at the core, the pugging process itself is not enough to prepare clay properly for use. To correctly align the particles, the clay must be wedged.

CLAY PARTICLE ORIENTATION PROBLEMS

These can arise in all making methods because each action on clay causes the long dimension of the plates to align perpendicularly to the forming pressure. Wheel-thrown items are especially at risk, making it very important to apply pressure to the base and sides as the form is pulled up to correctly align the particles.

Slip-cast wares are particularly prone to problems because the particles align themselves parallel to the mould face. Any faults in the mould surface affect the alignment, causing problems such as pronounced seams, which only become noticeable after firing. It is essential to maintain good mould quality and to replace them when worn to avoid these problems.

The difference in shrinkage rates between parallel and randomly orientated clay particles also leads to many drying problems. If, for instance, a wheel-thrown item is subsequently heavily turned, the correct alignment of particles at the surface of the form is cut away, leaving the more random arrangement at the centre. This automatically sets up strains in the clay wall, which can lead to cracks and warpage. Items with straight sides, such as mugs, cylinders, casseroles and storage jars, should therefore be turned as little as possible (if at all) to avoid problems.

Clay types: composition and nature

The first problem most makers encounter is deciding on the right clay for their work. There are many factors to consider, and clay suppliers offer a bewildering choice. The following generic clay types should help overcome the problem. Once you have found the type of clay to fit your requirements, ask your supplier for the closest match – for example: a grogged red clay with a wide firing range would be the terracotta sculpting clay, but the supplier will have others that fit the brief and will offer advice.

Terracotta

Terracotta is classed as earthenware clay and is found in large deposits all around the world. In its raw state, it can be any colour from ochre to red brown, depending on the type of organic matter and other impurities it contains. When fired, the colour can vary subtly from warm oranges to deep reds and browns, generally becoming darker the higher the clay is fired. The main colouring content of red clay is iron, which acts as a flux and determines the melting point of the clay. Terracottas can vary in firing range depending on their iron content, which, in turn, can differ significantly from one source to another – but generally all fire in the range 1020–1180°C (1940–2150°F).

   Manufactured terracottas come in a subtle range of textures and blends for all making methods for which red clay is preferred. It is also the cheapest clay because it is so readily and widely available.

Problems particularly associated with terracotta

SPALLING
Spalling manifests as areas of clay that appear to have sheared or flaked off the surface or rim of a form.

Caused by: Exposure to water and frost in low-fired, porous terracotta wares made for the outdoors.

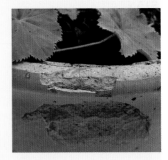

Solutions
- Wares cannot be saved once the damage is done, but reducing exposure by bringing such items indoors in the winter will reduce the problem.
- Make wares for outdoors in a higher-firing clay – red clays are available for firing at stoneware temperatures; clays that are fired to vitrification are less vulnerable because they are less porous.
- Use grogged clays for outdoor wares; an open grogged body is more robust for temperature extremes.

SCUMMING
White deposits on the surface or edges of dried and fired red clay wares.

Caused by: Soluble salts contained in the clay rising to the surface where the moisture gradient is greatest and the wares dry out fastest – on edges and rims.

Solutions
- If you are throwing wares, add a little vinegar to the water; if you are hand-building, try wiping over the surface of the wares with a vinegar-and-water solution before drying.
- Dry wares upside down so that the salts will form on the undersides, which are exposed to faster drying; the problem will be less evident here.
- Dry wares very slowly to distribute scumming more evenly and prevent concentration at the edges.

fired   unfired

fired

STANDARD TERRACOTTA

Colour: Unfired, dark brown/red; fired, warm orange/red
Firing temperature: 1020–1180°C (1940–2150°F)
Texture: Smooth, general-purpose clay
Suitable for: Throwing, coiling, hand-building, modelling, casting, machine-making
Commonly used for: Slip-decorated domestic wares and planters for the garden. However, terracotta does not fire high enough to vitrify completely, so it is subject to frost and water damage.

PROBLEMS

- Because of its high iron content, terracotta can contaminate white-clay pieces with a red colour.
- The high iron content means that when glazes are applied over a red body, the red iron colour may overwhelm the glaze.
- Crazing. This is unhygienic for functional wares, but otherwise not an issue. All low-fired glazed wares must be professionally tested for metal release before being used for domestic purposes.

SOLUTIONS

- Work with one clay type only or dedicate a space for working with red clay only, if possible. Clean up meticulously after use and change your apron or clothing when moving on to work with white clay.
- Apply a white slip over the clay at the leather-hard stage for a better colour response when applying glaze; see opposite, scumming, for examples of terracotta wares with white slip.
- Test to find the correct fit of glaze – one that will shrink at the same rate as the body to make it less porous. Many ceramic manufacturers have glazes specially made to fit their clays, but if you are using found clay, you will need to formulate your own glazes based on the clay's shrinkage rate.

FINE TERRACOTTA

Colour: Unfired, red/brown; as temperature increases, light red becoming darker
Firing temperature: 1080–1160°C (1976–2120°F)
Texture: Much finer than standard terracotta, for a very smooth finish
Suitable for: Throwing and machine-making
Commonly used for: Functional and domestic wares

PROBLEMS As for standard terracotta, see opposite

SOLUTIONS As for standard terracotta, see opposite

fired   unfired

TERRACOTTA, SCULPTURE

Colour: Unfired, red/brown; as temperature increases, pale red becoming darker
Firing temperature: 1020–1220°C (1868–2228°F)
Texture: Open textured containing medium to coarse grogs, but with good plasticity
Suitable for: Large-scale sculptural work, garden wares, slab work, etc.
Commonly used for: See 'suitable for'. Has good thermal shock resistance so is also suitable for raku and other low-fire techniques.

PROBLEM Not suitable for throwing, so difficult to make garden wares with this clay.

SOLUTION Make larger-scale garden wares by slabbing or coiling.

Clay types continued

fired

···

TERRACOTTA, GROGGED

···

Colour: Unfired, red/brown; as temperature increases, pale red becoming darker

Firing temperature: 1040–1160°C (1904–2120°F)

Texture: Medium–finely graded grogs

Suitable for: All types of production or studio-making methods, including throwing and machine-making and especially casting

Commonly used for: Functional and domestic wares, garden pots, etc.

PROBLEMS As for standard terracotta, see page 43

SOLUTIONS As for standard terracotta, see page 43

fired

···

TERRACOTTA, MOULDING CLAY

···

Colour: Unfired, red/brown; as temperature increases, pale red becoming darker

Firing temperature: 1020–1100°C (1868–2012°F)

Texture: Very coarse, but highly plastic

Suitable for: Modelling and sculptural work

Commonly used for: See 'suitable for'.

PROBLEMS
- Relatively low firing, so not suitable for outside wares unless glazed.
- Some coarser clay can be subject to lime popping because of the large amounts of grog contained in the body; see page 19.

SOLUTIONS
- To make outside wares, choose a higher-firing clay like the terracotta, sculpture.
- If lime popping is a real issue, consider changing the clay for one containing a different type of grog or try clay from another supplier.

▲ LICY CLAYDEN
This dramatic form has been coiled using black stoneware clay. The outer surface has been pared back to contrast with the fine porcelain slip used on the interior.

▲ BARRY STEDMAN
Wheel-thrown using earthenware clay, this form has been painted with coloured slips, stains and oxides and part glazed with a lead transparent glaze and fired to 1060°C (1940°F).

White earthenware

White earthenwares are commercially blended from ball clays and other minerals. They are generally chosen where a white background is desired for applying colour decoration.

WHITE EARTHENWARE, SMOOTH

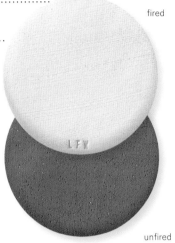

fired

unfired

Colour: Unfired, grey; fired, white
Firing temperature:
1060–1180°C
(1940–2150°F)
Texture: Smooth
Suitable for: Throwing, machine-making methods, slabbing (tile-making), slip casting
Commonly used for:
Functional domestic wares where a white body is required for good colour response

PROBLEMS

- Can be difficult to handle and is therefore not suitable for some forming techniques because of the fineness of texture and lack of plasticity.
- Crazing. It is difficult to match a glaze to a body type that will not craze.
- Has a strong clay memory, so any distortion during making, despite correction, will show up again during firing as warping or cracks.

SOLUTIONS

- Dry slowly and carefully away from direct extremes of temperature or air flow – especially where handles, lids, feet, etc., have been added to a main body – to reduce the risk.
- Crazing can be helped by biscuit firing to a higher temperature than the glaze firing.
- Handle as little as possible until the wares are leather hard or completely dry – especially slip-cast wares, which can be successfully fettled at this stage.

WHITE EARTHENWARE, GROGGED

Colour: Unfired, grey; fired, white
Firing temperature: 1080–1180°C (1976–2150°F)
Texture: Medium, using white grog to maintain body colour
Suitable for: Larger work – throwing, machine-making methods, slabbing, coiling (with care), tile-making
Commonly used for: Functional domestic wares, tile-making

PROBLEM Fewer problems and easier to handle, although still not as easy to work with as some other clays.

SOLUTION See smooth white earthenware, although a grogged version will always have better resistance to cracking and warping.

Black clays

Black clays can be bought commercially in varying textures from smooth to very coarse and usually have a wide firing range, making them suitable for both earthenware and stoneware treatments. To make them black, they contain very high proportions of oxide that act as a flux.

These clays are very plastic and can be used for all basic making techniques.

BLACK CLAY, SMOOTH

fired

unfired

Colour: Unfired, very dark red/brown; the higher the firing, dark brown to black
Firing temperature: 1080–1260°C (1976–2300°F)
Texture: Smooth, close texture and fine surface finish
Suitable for: Hand-building, sculpting, tile-making, relief panels, murals, throwing
Commonly used for: All and any of the above

PROBLEM Technically none, other than having to fire to the correct temperature, but this clay can be incredibly contaminating owing to its high oxide content; only really thorough cleaning will overcome the problem, but that can be very difficult because even the hands can be stained by this clay.

SOLUTION Work solely with either black or white clays or keep dedicated areas for using the two types – but be aware that clay carries on clothes as well as surfaces.

BLACK CLAY, CHUNKY

fired

Colour: Unfired, very dark red/brown; the higher the firing, dark brown to black
Firing temperature: 1080–1260°C (1976–2300°F)
Texture: Very coarse; low shrinkage
Suitable for: Big, rugged sculptural forms, architectural ceramics, large slab work
Commonly used for: All of the above

PROBLEMS See 'smooth black clay' for problems and solutions. Please note that black clay is also available in a smooth textured form, halfway between the two types above and with all the same features, and suitable for hand-building, sculpture work and large-scale throwing.

Clay types continued

Stonewares

Stoneware clay is fired considerably higher than earthenware clay – generally 1200–1300°C (2910–2370°F). As the temperature increases the body vitrifies, becomes largely nonporous and develops the appearance and qualities of stone, making it much stronger and more robust than earthenware. Commercially produced stonewares are blended with different grades of grog to provide a wide range of bodies from super-fine to extremely coarse.

fired   unfired

WIDE-FIRING WHITE STONEWARE

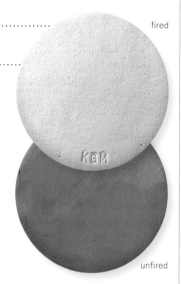

fired

Colour: Unfired, grey/buff; fired, warm cream
Firing temperature: 1080–1260°C (1976–2300°F)
Texture: Smooth or medium
Suitable for: Throwing, slabbing, hand-building, tile-making, slip casting
Commonly used for: Functional domestic wares, tile-making

PROBLEM Can speck slightly in reduction.
SOLUTION If specking is a problem, choose a different clay.

unfired

BUFF STONEWARE

Colour: Unfired, grey/buff; fired, grey/buff speckled grey
Firing temperature: 1180–1280°C (2156–2336°F)
Texture: Medium – fine mesh graded grogged
Suitable for: Throwing and hand-building, hand-modelling
Commonly used for: Functional domestic wares, hand-building, hand-modelling

PROBLEM None unless specific to maker; a good choice for general use.

fired

STONEWARE, RED-GROGGED

Colour: Unfired, red/brown; as temperature increases, rich red/brown becoming darker
Firing temperature: 1080–1220°C (1976–2228°F) high earthenware/ low stoneware
Texture: Coarse
Suitable for: Hand-building with good warp and crack resistance
Commonly used for: Large sculptural work

PROBLEMS As with all grogged bodies, there can be some problems with lime popping at lower temperatures.
SOLUTION Little can be done if lime popping occurs, but speak to your clay supplier for advice if the problem persists.

▼ There are many varied stoneware clays to choose from; these samples demonstrate a range of fired colours, each possessing its own characteristics.

fired   B 17C 6   unfired

WHITE STONEWARE, GROGGED

Colour: Unfired, grey/buff; fired, pale buff/ cream

Firing temperature: 1220–1280°C (2228–2336°F)

Texture: Medium – fine mesh graded grogged

Suitable for: Throwing, slabbing, hand-building, tile-making

Commonly used for: Functional domestic wares, tile-making, hand-building

PROBLEMS None unless specific to maker; a good choice for decorative colour treatments.

fired   DELTA

SPECKLED STONEWARE

Colour: Unfired, dark grey; fired, light buff to grey with strong speckle

Firing temperature: 1120–1280°C (2048–2336°F)

Texture: Fine

Suitable for: Throwing, modelling, casting

Commonly used for: Functional domestic wares

PROBLEM Speckle will appear through glaze under oxidizing conditions, but this is usually a chosen feature of the clay.

▲ ANDREW ADAIR
The form has been thrown using stoneware clay then soft porcelain has been smeared over the surface before being artificially dried with a blow torch and then thrown again to create the surface detail.

fired   EX? 50   unfired

STONEWARE, GROGGED

Colour: Unfired, grey; in oxidation, toasted buff; under reduction, warm speckled orange buff

Firing temperature: 1160–1300°C (2120–2372°F)

Texture: Coarse

Suitable for: Hand-building and sculpting, with good green strength, warp and crack resistance; raku firing

Commonly used for: Hand-building, sculptural work, murals, raku

PROBLEMS As with all grogged bodies, there can be some problems with lime popping.

SOLUTION Little can be done if lime popping occurs, but speak to your clay supplier for advice if the problem persists.

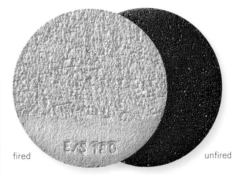

fired   E/S 180   unfired

STONEWARE, EXTRA-GROGGED SCULPTING OR PIZZA BODY

Colour: Unfired, dark grey; fired, warm buff to grey

Firing temperature: 900–1280°C (1652–2336°F)

Texture: Very coarse

Suitable for: Pizza ovens, raku, large sculptures, saggers and hand-building. Warp and crack resistant; low shrinkage; good thermal shock

Commonly used for: Large sculptural work, pizza ovens, saggers

PROBLEM Because of the very large particle size of grog, there can be some spit-out.

SOLUTION Spit-out does not affect the overall effectiveness of the final products made using this clay. Alternatively, choose a clay with a finer grog.

▲ CHIU-I WU
This charming sculpture has been made from stoneware clay. Nothing has been added by way of decoration – the form's serenity is derived from this simplicity.

Porcelain

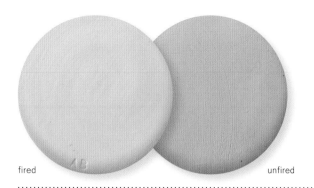

fired   unfired

Porcelains are the whitest clay bodies available, but even so the quality of whiteness can vary considerably from different sources. Recent developments have created some truly beautiful, startlingly white bodies with amazingly translucent qualities. Generally, the whiter the porcelain fires, the more it costs to buy.

Porcelain is not highly plastic and it takes much practice and perseverance to gain experience in handling it. Generally fired above 1250°C (2280°F), there can be problems with cracking and distortion as the clay reaches vitrification, but, when fired successfully, it is very strong and durable, which is why it is used so extensively in manufacturing and for industrial purposes.

Porcelain shrinks between 15 and 18 per cent from dry to vitrified — the greatest shrinkage of all clays; this is something to consider when planning and designing wares.

STANDARD PORCELAIN

Colour: Unfired, creamy white; fired, white and translucent
Firing temperature: 1220–1280°C (2228–2336°F)
Texture: Very smooth
Suitable for: Throwing, modelling, hand-building, casting
Commonly used for: Throwing and casting domestic and decorative wares

PROBLEMS

■ Generally difficult to handle, quickly going from soft to leather hard and dry — often before construction is complete.

● Easily distorted at the making stage due to the fact that porcelain is generally worked in thin sections, resulting in warping and cracking in firing.

SOLUTIONS

■ Only practice and experimentation will overcome difficulties in handling. If they cannot be overcome, try a more plastic clay such as semi-porcelain, which fires to a slightly lower temperature.

● Make all parts to be joined at the same time to minimize different shrinkage rates. Dry wares very slowly, under cover, especially where parts have been added on.

▼ CLAIRE PALASTANGA
This incredibly delicate sculpture has been made using porcelain. Claire is intrigued by process and believes that the mistakes and errors made when working in clay are as important (if not more so) as the end result. She believes they are all part of the journey.

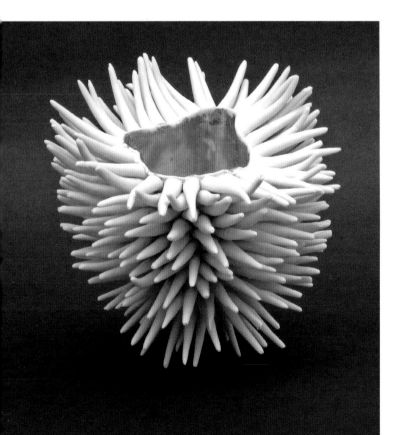

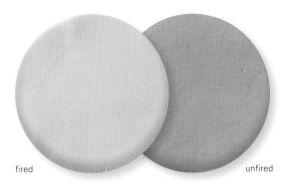

fired   unfired

SUPER-WHITE PORCELAIN

Colour: Unfired, blue/white; fired, bright white, glasslike translucency
Firing temperature: 1250–1280°C (2282–2336°F)
Texture: Very smooth
Suitable for: Throwing, modelling, hand-building
Commonly used for: Throwing domestic and decorative wares, fine slab work

PROBLEM There are fewer problems associated with this type of porcelain because it is made from low iron-bearing china clays, silicas, bentonites and mineral fluxes, which make it much more plastic than standard porcelain. The major problem here is mainly cost because it is generally more expensive.

SOLUTION Use efficiently to minimize waste and recycle all scrap.

fired

PORCELAIN CASTING CLAY

Colour: Unfired, white; fired, white and translucent
Firing temperature: 1220–1280°C (2228–2336°F)
Texture: Smooth – liquid
Suitable for: Casting domestic and decorative wares, figurines, etc.
Commonly used for: Domestic and decorative wares

PROBLEM High shrinkage.

SOLUTION Plan the mould size carefully to accommodate the shrinkage rate when casting.

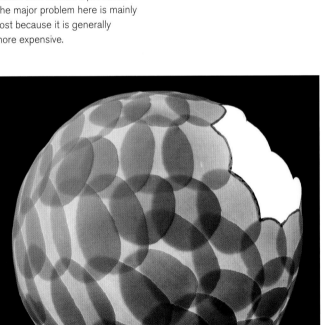

◄ DIEDERICK HEYNING
Using Southern Ice (a type of super-white porcelain) mixed with flax fibres for handling strength, this form has been constructed from slab-rolled sections, assembled and formed in a plaster mould then fired in reduction to 1260°C (2300°F) in a stoneware mould to avoid sagging.

Bone china

Bone china is made from calcined animal bone or bone ash, Cornish stone and china clay. The bone forms approximately half of the body and acts as a flux to produce an almost glasslike, pure white, translucent and very hard material when fired above 1250°C (2282°F). If you are buying bone china clay that has been commercially produced, follow the manufacturer's recommended firing temperature for best results.

Unlike other clays, bone china is fired to its top temperature at the biscuit stage, which can be problematic in that it does not have a very wide maturing range (the maturing point refers to the temperature at which the clay becomes hard and durable – for most clays there is often a small range of temperatures between which this can happen – firing beyond the maturing range can cause the clay to warp or sag) so it can easily distort and lose its shape. This is usually overcome by supporting or setting the wares for the biscuit firing. The subsequent glaze firing is usually low – 1000–1080°C (1832–1976°F) – making it unnecessary to support the work again given that it has already been fired to vitrification.

Plastic bone china recipe

Basic recipe for a plastic bone china body if wishing to mix from raw materials.

Bone ash   50%
China clay   25%
Cornish stone   25%

Please note that small amounts of ball clay i.e. 1–2% can be added to increase strength and plasticity, but will affect colour slightly; otherwise this is a dense, white vitreous (less than 1% water) translucent body.

Casting times: 2–3 minutes for 3 mm (⅛ in) thickness

Glazing: Because the clay vitrifies in the high biscuit range, application of glaze can be difficult. Either heat the wares beforehand or add 1–2% gum arabic to the glaze to aid adhesion.

BONE CHINA

Colour: Unfired, white; fired in thin form, white and translucent
Firing temperature: High biscuit – 1250–1260°C (2282–2300°F); Low glaze – 1000–1080°C (1832–1976°F)
Texture: Smooth – liquid
Suitable for: Casting domestic and decorative wares, figurines, etc.
Commonly used for: Domestic and decorative wares

fired

PROBLEMS

■ High shrinkage on firing (up to 15 per cent).

● Bodies can go 'off-colour' – that is, lose their whiteness and translucency – because of the addition of ball clay to improve plasticity; ball clay is iron bearing, so even the low-iron varieties can have a colouring effect.

◆ The short firing range leads to considerable warping. This happens when the body reaches its eutectic temperature (the lowest melting point of two or more substances) and becomes pyroplastic (up to 40 per cent of the total body) at this point. There may only be as little as 5°C (41°F) difference between the optimum temperature and the body overfiring and slumping or sagging.

SOLUTIONS

■ Make models for your plaster mould approximately 12 per cent larger than the desired finished size.

● Remove or reduce the ball clay content to no more than 1–2 per cent.

◆ Reduce the top temperature by 10°C (18°F) to 1250°C (2282°F) and soak for 1½ hours.

▼ ANGELA MELLOR
Inspiration for this delicate form has been drawn from marine life. The bowl has been slip cast in bone china and textured paper clay has been added to create the imagery in the upper section.

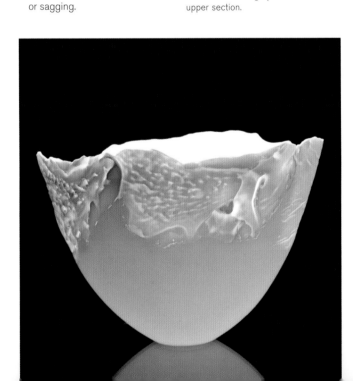

Paper clays

Commercially made paper clays contain finely chopped fibres of flax and cellulose, which give the clay strength and flexibility as well as making it very lightweight. This type of clay has revolutionized making methods in recent times because the fibre content produces an internal structure with a capillary system that transfers moisture easily and evenly through the clay, allowing sections to be joined very easily at any stage of making; even green sections can be joined to bone-dry parts and the form will be unbelievably strong, easy to handle and even transportable. I know of one potter who carried bone-dry paper-clay slabs halfway across the world in a suitcase to assemble them at a demonstration workshop – and having constructed the form, then carried it off the stage by a handle he had added. Amazing!

The clay is suitable for many making methods and can easily be made in the studio using your own clay in earthenware, stoneware or porcelain. Recipes and making methods are available on the Internet and in many books.

On a minor note, paper clay feels and handles slightly differently to other clay types and breaks all the construction rules, so it takes a little getting used to.

fired

unfired

PAPER CLAYS

Colour: PORCELAIN: Unfired, creamy white; fired, pure white BUFF STONEWARES: Unfired, grey; fired, buff and warm buff

Firing temperature: 1240°C (2264°F); in grogged form, 1280°C (2336°F)

Texture: Smooth to coarse owing to cellulose content and grog

Suitable for: Slab work, figurative sculpture, hand-building, throwing (with practice), and a range of firing types including raku, oxidation, reduction, salt and soda.

Commonly used for: Slab work and figurative sculpture

PROBLEMS

■ There are health and safety issues around the storage of paper clay because it rots and smells if stored for too long and forms dangerous mould.

● Firing of paper clay creates extra smoke and fumes.

SOLUTIONS

■ Add a capful of bleach when mixing your paper clay. Make it in small batches that can be used up in one or two weeks. You can scrape surface mould off and use the clay safely, but if the mould has penetrated and the clay is black inside, it must be thrown away.

● Allow extra ventilation when firing paper clay – especially in the first few hundred degrees of the firing.
Please note that commercially bought paper clays are less prone to mould growth.

Paper clay filler method

One of the most amazing things about paper clay is that it can be used as a filler to mend splits and cracks in biscuit-fired wares – even ones that have been made from your usual clay.

To make up the paper clay filler:
Make the paper pulp in the recommended way, then blend with your dry clay, using distilled white vinegar instead of water to bind the mixture to the right consistency. Keep some of the mixture in slip form for the edges of the damaged form, but firm up the rest to a workable state to use in soft coils to fill gaps.

When the paper clay has dried, it can be sanded back carefully and the form re-biscuit fired before applying glaze or other treatments.

Fired buff stonewares

Clay preparation

Reclaiming

THE PROBLEM

Excess water after slaking down

Caused by: Result of the reclaiming process. As clay particles slake down, they sink to the bottom of the container, leaving excess water above.

THE SOLUTIONS

Good routine: Reclaim clay in smaller quantities to make handling easier. Put excess clay directly into the container you will reclaim in, then you will know when it is time to process another batch. This way, you will keep on top of it and save money and time.

Break up dry clay: To make the clay easier to slake down, put the bone-dry clay into a tough plastic bag and tie loosely to prevent the clay escaping, then, using a wooden mallet, smash the clay into smaller pieces or dust if preferred, before adding to water.

Use hot water: The clay will slake down much faster and more thoroughly in hot water.

Remove excess water
- Start by removing the bulk of the water with a jug.
- Remove the remaining excess water with a pipette or slip-trailing bulb (left); it can be slow, but is efficient in removing pockets of water.

A sponge can be used to soak up excess water.

Firming clay for wedging

THE PROBLEM

Clay is too sloppy to handle

Caused by: This is a natural result of the reclaiming process. When all excess water has been removed, the clay is still in a very sloppy state.

THE SOLUTIONS

Spread over a plaster bat: Spread the clay evenly over a plaster bat or absorbent board and allow it to firm up. When the clay in contact with the plaster surface has firmed up to a point where it can be handled, turn the clay over to allow the rest to firm up.

Pour into a cloth bag: Pour the wet clay into a cloth bag contained within a plastic bin. Suspend the handles of the bag over the handles of the bin or from a higher point, so that the excess water can drain through the cloth and collect in the bottom. Depending on atmospheric conditions, the clay may take hours or a couple of days to firm up to the required level for wedging.

Use a bin that is deeper than the bag when it is suspended – it will allow the water to drain away more freely.

Spread the clay as evenly as possible over the plaster bat.

Wedging

Try to keep the shape as neat as possible when wedging – it prevents air from being introduced accidentally.

THE PROBLEM

Air trapped in the clay after wedging

Despite thorough wedging air pockets remain in the clay, showing up as the clay block is cut through.

Caused by: Incorrect wedging, or organic or other materials being trapped in the clay.

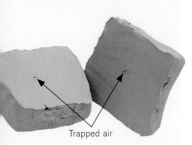

Trapped air

THE SOLUTIONS

Correct wedging method
1 Form the clay into a block that is comfortable to handle; 4–4.5 kg (9–10 lb) is a good starting weight.
2 Form the clay into a square or oblong. This shape will give you more control.
3 Lift the clay and drop one end onto the wedging bench.
4 Cut through the clay with a wire from the underside to form two halves.
5 Lift one half of the block, turn it over, then throw it forcibly onto the half still on the bench. This action will force out the air.
6 Reshape the block and repeat the process until all air pockets are removed.

Remove and prevent contaminents
■ Remove foreign bodies from the clay if they appear; organic material will fire out, but other materials can cause problems later.
■ Make sure that the working area is clean and free of contaminants.

Ox-head kneading

THE PROBLEM

Trapped air

Air is introduced into the clay rather than eliminated as the clay is kneaded.

Caused by: Poor technique: too much clay is turned over in the kneading process, trapping air in the folds.

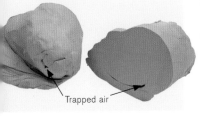

Trapped air

THE SOLUTION

Good kneading technique
1 Position your hands at opposite sides of the clay mass, with your fingers wrapped around the sides.
2 Push the clay down and away from you; as you do this, a raised mass will remain in the centre.
3 Roll the clay back towards you and reposition your hands slightly forward, then repeat the process. Do not try to move great masses of clay each time; it should be done in small, repeated motions, so that the clay does not fold over on itself but each movement blends the clay with the one before.
4 Continue to rock and push the clay until it is smooth, with no air pockets.

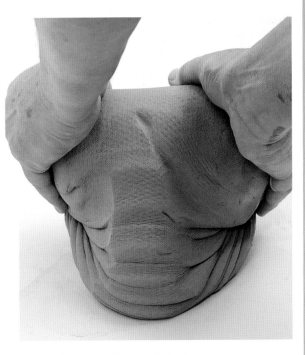

Keep the clay contained between the hands by applying a slight inward pressure.

Spiral kneading

THE PROBLEM

The difficulty of the method

Air is introduced in the process of kneading, since the method is the most difficult to perform.

Caused by: Working with too much clay to handle comfortably; poor technique; clay is too firm.

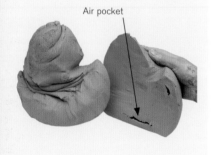

Air pocket

THE SOLUTION

Air removal technique
This is a method of removing air from clay and making the clay more workable by redistributing the water content. It is much easier if the clay is on the soft side because the process can also firm the clay up.
1 Place your hands on opposite sides of a roughly rounded lump of clay that you can handle comfortably.
2 Push down on the clay with your right hand while rolling it forward, using your left hand to contain the clay and prevent sideways movement. Rotate the clay with your left hand after each movement.
3 Continue to rotate the clay anticlockwise, moving the right hand into position for each downward push.
4 Work rhythmically in such a way as to avoid turning large areas of clay over onto itself and trapping air in the folds. Cut through the clay periodically to check your progress.

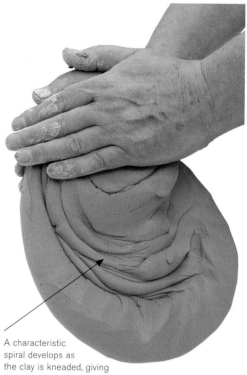

A characteristic spiral develops as the clay is kneaded, giving the technique its name.

Clay is too wet

THE PROBLEM

Sloppy and sticky clay

The clay sticks to the hands, won't hold its shape and has a high shrinkage rate.

Caused by: Poor processing after reclaiming; storing in wet conditions; excessive carbonaceous or organic content.

THE SOLUTIONS

Allow to firm up: Re-spread the clay over a plaster bat and allow it to firm up, then wedge or knead it to a workable consistency.
Wedge with coarser clay: The clay may be what is referred to as fat clay, meaning that it is too plastic. If this is the case, wedge the wet clay with a coarser type containing nonplastic kaolins or fireclay in alternate layers until you have a workable plastic body **(1)**. Test the clay for shrinkage and performance before committing to using it.
Reduce bentonite: If you are mixing your own clay, try either using no bentonite or reducing the bentonite content and decreasing the amount of ball clay.
Leave clay to mature: After processing, store the clay in a dry, well-ventilated area away from extremes of temperature and leave to mature for four to 10 weeks.

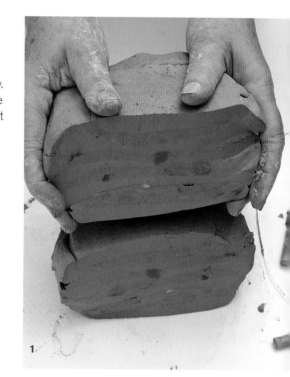

1

Clay is too dry

THE PROBLEM

Clay is too firm to work

The clay is not completely dried out but too firm to work with and lacking plasticity.

Caused by: Poor storage with exposure to heat or air.

THE SOLUTIONS

Wedge with softer clay: The best way to save dry clay from the reclaiming bin is to layer it with much softer clay and wedge the two together to a workable body. This is a useful way of processing reclaimed clay that can be quite wet.

Wrap in damp towel: Alternatively, wrap the clay in a damp or wet towel inside a plastic bag and leave for a day or two to soften up.

Submerge in water: Try also piercing holes through the bag containing the clay and into the clay itself, then submerge the bag in a bucket of water and leave for anything from 30 minutes to 24 hours, testing by squeezing regularly to check progress. Reseal the clay in a hole-free bag to store.

Here you can clearly see the harder clay in layers with reconstituted clay containing lumps not yet thoroughly mixed in.

Testing for plasticity

Left: good plastic body. **Centre:** body with a larger grog content, which naturally reduces plasticity, but only marginally in this case, making it still workable. **Right:** porcelain body (notorious for its lack of plasticity) that has cracked significantly in curling; this would be difficult to use.

THE PROBLEM

Clay lacking plasticity

Clay is unworkable and seems unfit for the chosen purpose.

Caused by: Choosing the wrong type of clay; the ratio of water to clay is too low; the clay has been poorly prepared or not matured for long enough (significant in reclaimed clay); the body has been made using acidic water.

THE SOLUTIONS

Test plasticity: Test the clay by rolling out a coil about as thick as a finger, then curl it around a pencil or thin tube. If the clay curls easily without cracks, it is a good plastic body suitable for hand-building or throwing.

To make nonplastic clay workable
■ Reclaim it to a softer, more workable consistency (see page 52, problems associated with reclaiming clay: clay too dry).
■ Wedge with layers of softer clay to increase the water content.

■ Allow reclaimed clay to mature for longer – four to 10 weeks.
■ Use water with mild acidity when mixing or reclaiming. A pH of 6.5 is best (tap water).

Mixing your own clay: Try mixing 1–2 per cent bentonite into the clay, adding ball clay or more plastic kaolin, and otherwise decreasing nonplastic ingredients.

CHAPTER 3 FORMING

AND BISCUIT WARE

IF PROBLEMS APPEAR AT THE CONSTRUCTION STAGE OF MAKING, IT IS VITALLY IMPORTANT THAT THEY ARE REMEDIED QUICKLY TO AVOID FURTHER PROBLEMS IN FIRING. THIS CHAPTER WORKS THROUGH MANY OF THE COMMON PROBLEMS ENCOUNTERED, WITH CLEAR IMAGES OF THE FAULTS AND WAYS TO FIX THEM.

Forming

The secret to avoiding many problems when forming lies in good preparation, attention to detail and making sure you have the right tools. It is assumed here that you will already have the basic making skills necessary to work in clay – but when things go wrong, it can often be enough to go back to the basics of best practice to find out where the problem arose.

Clay preparation

For any forming method, you must prepare the clay by wedging and kneading it to remove air pockets, excess water and so on. If the clay has been through a de-airing pug mill, you can bypass this process – but it is still important to know the techniques of wedging and kneading in order to process smaller amounts of clay.

WEDGING

This is the best way of removing excess air; it is also a useful way of combining different clays, mixing hard and soft clays to make a working body and preparing large lumps ready for use.

Process: Form the clay into a rectangular block; if you are mixing two or more clays, layer them alternatively in a stack. Lift the block with a hand and drop one end onto the workbench. Draw a cutting wire through the clay from the underside of the block to divide it in two. Lift one half and turn through 90°, then slam it back down onto the block on the bench. Pick up the whole block, rotate through 90° again and repeat the process at least

five times – or, if combining different clays, until they are thoroughly mixed together.

OX-HEAD KNEADING

So called because the shape that is formed in the process looks much like an ox's head, this is a way of firming wet clay up as well as de-airing and homogenizing it.

Process: Make sure the clay is malleable enough to handle with ease. Form the clay into a ball, then place your hands on either side of the ball and push the clay forward, away from your body, while at the same time applying inward pressure to prevent the clay from spreading outward. Roll the lump back towards your body, then push back again; the ox-head shape will form as the process is repeated.

SPIRAL KNEADING

This is an easier method of kneading for larger lumps of clay.

Process: Again, the clay needs to be relatively soft to process successfully. Form it into a rough ball,

▲ **Wedging** This method is a useful way of mixing big lumps of clay. The name is derived from cutting the block at an angle into a wedge shape.

▲ **Ox-head** This type of kneading is best used for small to medium amounts of clay.

▲ **Spiral** If you are working with a large amount of clay, this is a useful kneading technique.

then with one hand push down on one side, roll the ball forward and push down again, using your other hand to keep the shape from splaying out. As the process is repeated, the ball will become cone shaped, with an obvious spiral at the top.

Forming methods

Many problems can be completely avoided by simply paying attention to detail when forming – making sure seams are properly joined or that coils are well blended together, for instance. This section presents the pros and cons for each forming method, with tips for best practice and suggestions for tools and equipment to help you get the most out of your preferred technique.

COILING

ADVANTAGES
- Relatively few tools are required, so it is a process that can be mastered with minimum outlay.
- It is a contemplative, slow method of working that can produce organic, sculptural forms or finely controlled wares with many uses, from the purely decorative to tablewares or garden pots.
- Forms of any size can be produced; the size is limited only by the size of your kiln – and even then, forms can be made in sections to be joined after firing.

DISADVANTAGES
- It is difficult to exactly replicate a form using this technique, even if you are using outline formers to keep the shape. However, this makes each piece unique.

ESSENTIAL TOOLS AND EQUIPMENT
- A good-sized, nonabsorbent surface for rolling and flattening coils
- Plastic sheeting for flattening coils or rolling clay for a slabbed or moulded base
- A wooden bat for working on
- A whirler for turning the form as the coils are applied.
- Wooden or plastic modelling tools for blending coils
- Scraping tools – kidneys, surform blades
- A potter's or craft knife

HELPFUL TOOLS
- An old toothbrush or a brush for applying slip
- A potter's pin
- A hairdryer
- Outline template and/or formers for keeping shapes true
- Hump and/or press moulds to use for exposed coil forms and as bases to coil onto

GENERAL TIPS
- Whether you are constructing with rounded or flattened coils, the secret to success lies in preparing the coils well, to the same size, thickness and shape.

- Prepare several coils to speed things up. Once prepared, keep them under plastic until ready to use to prevent moisture loss.

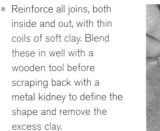

- Join flattened coils together by scoring and slipping each edge thoroughly (use a toothbrush and water as an alternative; this does both jobs in one).

- Reinforce all joins, both inside and out, with thin coils of soft clay. Blend these in well with a wooden tool before scraping back with a metal kidney to define the shape and remove the excess clay.

- If the form starts to distort, add temporary coils inside for support. These can be left in place if not visible when complete to aid the firing process.

- Use a pin to check the thickness of the clay wall periodically; scrape away excess with a kidney to keep the clay section even at all times.

PINCHING

ADVANTAGES

- This is the oldest, most tried and tested way of working in clay.
- Few tools and little equipment are required.
- The technique can be used to make anything from vessels to sculptural, multifaceted forms.
- Pinched sections can be coiled, slabbed or modelled onto.

DISADVANTAGES

- Pinched forms are generally small in size because the technique is limited to a large extent by the size of the maker's hands – although shapes can be extended by coiling and then pinching or slabbing onto a base shape.

ESSENTIAL TOOLS AND EQUIPMENT

- Scraping and smoothing tools – metal, plastic and rubber kidneys and/or ribs
- A knife or surform for levelling edges
- A wooden bat or board for placing work on once formed
- An old toothbrush or a brush for applying slip when joining sections
- A potter's pin for measuring the thickness of the clay wall
- Soft plastic sheeting for storing work in progress

HELPFUL TOOLS

- A hairdryer
- A whirler
- Foam or sponge pads for supporting work in progress, drying difficult shapes, etc.

▲ GABRIELE KOCH
This piece has been hand-built using both pinching and coiling. The surface was painted with slip and burnished several times before firing. The pattern is the result of a carefully organized smoke-firing in sawdust.

GENERAL TIPS

- Soft clay is easier to pinch than hard clay because excessive handling has a drying effect.

- Hot hands dry clay really quickly, causing cracks and other problems. Cool your hands down in cold water periodically to prevent overdrying.

- Learn the technique in stages, starting with small balls of clay and working up in size as you gain control.

- Pinch the base shape of the form first because once the sides have been raised it is difficult and ultimately impossible to stretch the fingers back.

- If the shape starts to feel floppy, rest it in an inverted position to allow the clay to firm up a little. Alternatively, dry it off slightly with a hairdryer – but be careful not to overdry.

THROWING

ADVANTAGES
- Production is faster – many more items can be produced in a day.
- Shapes can be repeated accurately.
- Good for making a wide range of items, from domestic wares to garden pots.

DISADVANTAGES
- It takes much longer to properly master the technique of throwing.
- Equipment is more expensive.
- More work and storage space is required to accommodate larger production.
- Kiln turnover is greater owing to greater production.
- Larger amounts of clay are required.

ESSENTIAL TOOLS AND EQUIPMENT
- Wheel
- Water bowl
- Sponges
- Cutting wire
- A potter's pin or needle
- A potter's knife
- Callipers
- Selection of ribs

HELPFUL TOOLS
- Wheel head designed for throwing bats
- Boards for placing thrown items onto
- Custom-made tools – individual to each maker

GENERAL TIPS

- Knead the clay well before throwing, using one of the recommended methods.
- Choose the right clay: smooth clay for delicate, smaller items; medium-textured clay for tableware, ovenware and larger pots; coarse clay for garden pots or those that need to withstand thermal shock, such as those that are raku fired, for example.

- Weigh clay for batch throwing to maintain equal size.

- Store prepared balls of clay in a plastic bowl, covered with a sheet of plastic to stop them drying out before throwing.
- Make sure everything you will need is at hand before beginning.

SLABBING

ADVANTAGES
- Slabbed surfaces provide great opportunity for creative decoration.
- Slabbing is a controlled way of working with easily repeatable outcomes.
- Few tools and little equipment are required.
- Any scale forms can be made, from tiny porcelain boxes to large, outdoor sculptures and garden planters.

DISADVANTAGES
- Slabbed forms are prone to warping and splitting at the seams.

ESSENTIAL TOOLS AND EQUIPMENT
- Large rolling pin, preferably straight, without handles
- Pairs of roller guides in varying thicknesses and lengths for different types of construction
- Plastic sheeting for rolling slabs
- A potter's knife for cutting slabs and mitres, scoring, etc.
- An old toothbrush or brushes for applying slip
- A wooden bat for working on – or a kiln shelf for large-scale items

HELPFUL TOOLS
- A whirler (for smaller-scale wares)
- A slab roller for making large-scale items where big slabs are required
- Cardboard templates of all sections of the form to be made; this saves having to measure each section individually

GENERAL TIPS
- Choose the right clay. The scale of the piece will generally determine the most suitable type, but as a general rule, smaller works can be made in almost any clay, while large-scale works need a clay body with tooth, so a grogged body would be recommended. Also bear in mind that if the form is to be sited outside, then the clay will need to have weatherproof qualities. Manufacturers' catalogues are usually a good guide for making the right choice.

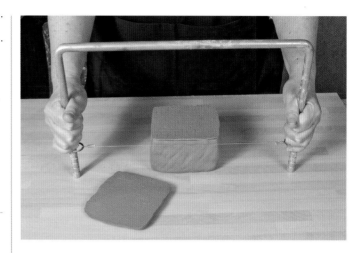

- Prepare all slabs for a form at the same time, to avoid having to join sections that are at different stages of dryness.

- Allow slabs for firm-wall constructions to dry to almost leather hard before joining.

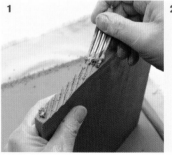
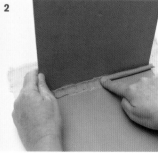

- Always score and slip joining edges and reinforce with soft coils of clay on the inside of the form. (**1** and **2**)
- If you want to make large-scale slabbed wares, it may be helpful to invest in a slab roller.
- If possible, work on the kiln shelf on which the item will be fired to avoid having to handle the form too much once completed.

SLIP CASTING AND MOULD MAKING

ADVANTAGES

- Forms can be exactly replicated.
- This is the best process for production wares that need to be produced quickly.

DISADVANTAGES

- Larger workspace is required to accommodate moulds and the working process itself.
- It is a much more formulaic way of working: the creative element of slip casting lies in the design of the moulds and the surface decoration of wares.
- Ideally, there should be a separate room for plaster work to avoid contamination of the clay.
- More tools and equipment are required.

ESSENTIAL TOOLS AND EQUIPMENT

More tools are required for model and mould making than for casting.

- Plastic bin with lid for storage of plaster
- Buckets and basins for mixing plaster
- Jugs – for measuring liquids and for pouring slip into moulds
- Weighing scales
- Spoons and whisks for mixing small amounts of plaster
- Cottling materials for round and irregular shapes: flexible and transparent high-density plastic sheeting, linoleum, soft clay, roofing lead
- Cottling materials for square or rectangular forms: wooden boards, soft clay, plaster bats
- Materials for securing cottles: pegs, string, soft clay, wooden wedges
- Soft soap
- Soft bristle brushes
- Natural sponges
- Plaster-turning tools and chisels – for making models
- Scrapers and metal kidneys
- Surform blades for carving and reducing surface
- Hacksaw blades – indispensible for modelling
- Rifflers for detailed carving

HANDY TOOLS – MACHINERY

- Plaster turning lathe for creating round, symmetrical models
- Bench whirler for making flatwares such as plates. It allows the excess clay to be turned off the exterior of moulds and for a recess to be turned into the base of moulds for a foot ring.
- Bandsaw for cutting flat forms out of plaster bats when making handles.
- Blunger for mixing large amounts of casting slip from powdered or plastic clay.

◄ Fettling knife, mould-maker's knife and mould trimming knife.

► Spring callipers.

◄ Sieves with differing mesh sizes.

MISCELLANEOUS TOOLS

- Rasps, files and knives for finishing models and moulds
- Wet-and-dry sandpaper – grade 240–1000 – for finishing plaster surfaces and fettling cast surfaces
- Callipers for measuring dimensions
- Indelible pencils for marking centre and guide lines on a form
- Compasses for dividing a model to find the centre line
- Coins used for making natches
- Rubber mallet – for releasing models from moulds
- Steel hammer for splitting moulds
- Inner tubes for holding moulds together when casting
- Steel square for finding the perpendicular surface
- Dottle sponges for softening edges after casting
- Paintbrushes for applying slip to join sections such as handles
- Sieves – 60-mesh – for preparing slip
- Small spirit level for finding true surface
- Straight edges and metal rulers for screeding large areas of plaster

GENERAL TIPS

PLASTER WORK

- Keep all plaster work separate from clay work, preferably in a separate room. Be meticulous in clearing up to avoid clay contamination and subsequent explosions in firing.
- Do not put plaster down the sink drain; it will set and block it.
- Store plaster in a dry area, contained in a sealable plastic bin at a temperature no lower than 13°C (55°F).
- Use plaster within three months.
- As a general guide when mixing plaster, use two parts water to three parts plaster. **(1)**
- Add the plaster to water, not water to the plaster. **(2)**
- Use water at room temperature.
- Allow the plaster to stand for 1–2 minutes before mixing to allow it to saturate properly.
- Stir the mixture in one direction only. Do not remove your hand until the mixture is at the right pouring consistency. This will help to avoid introducing air. **(3)**
- Make sure the model is close at hand when mixing the plaster to avoid having to carry the heavy weight. Also, once the plaster is ready to pour, it can set really quickly so the model needs to be at a comfortable height for pouring. **(4)**
- Dry moulds slowly in a drying cupboard; avoid drying on top of the kiln, since this can cause the plaster to crack.
- Store moulds in a dry place.

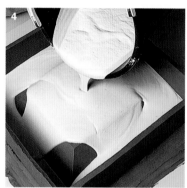

SLIP CASTING

- Before casting, make sure that moulds are free from dust, old bits of clay left from previous castings and so on.
- If you are using a new mould, discard the first casting because it may have picked up bits of plaster left over from when the mould was made.
- Pour the slip in a steady flow, directing it towards the centre of the base of the mould. **(1)**
- Pouring slip into the mould through a cooking sieve will help avoid a casting spot (a hard spot in the cast, which can be resistant to glaze).
- Rotate large moulds on a banding wheel when pouring slip to avoid filling lines.
- After casting, pour the slip out in a steady flow, circulating the mould as you pour.
- Drain the mould at an angle of 30–40°. **(2)**
- Fettle the cast forms at the leather-hard stage, using a fettling knife or scalpel and sponge. **(3 and 4)**
- Join component parts – handles, spouts and so on – at a compatible stage of leather hardness to avoid cracks and distortions.
- Use casting slip mixed with water to stick parts together; casting slip will not work on its own because it is too thick.

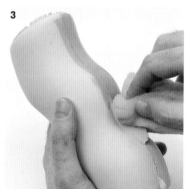
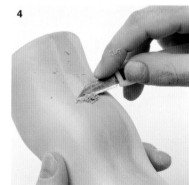

MEASURING PINT WEIGHT

- Pint weight is critical because it determines whether or not the slip works correctly. Casting slip needs a very specific ratio of solids to water, along with a deflocculant, to work properly. Once you have established a slip that works well for you, measure the pint weight and keep a record of it so that it can be repeated exactly.

METHOD: CHOOSE A NARROW-NECKED CONTAINER.

- Weigh it empty, then return the scales to zero.
- Weigh a pint of casting slip in the container.
- If the weight is too high compared to the original mix, add water. If it is too low, add dry materials or clay until the weight is back to your original.
- There are no definitive weights to use as a guide because the slip will be pertinent to the maker and their choice of clay, etc., but once established and recorded, you will always have a point of reference.
- Pint weight can then be used in conjunction with Brongniart's formula to calculate additions of body stains to make coloured casting slips.

BRONGNIART'S FORMULA

- Density measurements are essential for the accurate control of casting and other slips plus slop glazes. Use Brongniart's formula to determine how much dry material is suspended in your clay slip or glaze so that additions can be added as a percentage. For example: If you wanted to add say 1% cobalt to your slip or glaze to colour it pale blue you would measure 1 pint of slip, apply Brongniart's formula then add the cobalt at 1% of dry content.

$$W = \frac{(p - 20) \times g}{g - 1}$$

Where W = oz of dry material in one pint of slip
g = specific gravity of dry material (usually 2.5 for clays)
p = pint weight in oz of one pint of slip

$$W = \frac{(p - 1000) \times g}{g - 1}$$

Where W = grams of dry material in one litre of slip
g = specific gravity of dry material (usually 2.5 for clays)
p = pint weight in grams of one litre of slip

The measurement of pint weight is also critical for glazes, to establish a repeatable outcome.

▼ MAREK CECULA
Natural stone was used to make the models for this inspired tea set. The forms are slip cast in porcelain then industrial china parts added for handles, spout and lid. The set has been simply decorated using ceramic decals.

Drying considerations

Clay needs water to make it plastic and highly plastic clays require much more water than coarse-grained types. It follows, therefore, that individual clays will dry at varying speeds. Drying time is also affected by other factors, such as atmosphere and the thickness of the clay wall. It is important to bear in mind that drying should always be even and controlled.

What happens in the drying process?

In simple terms, drying occurs as water evaporates from the surface of wares, but there is also a deeper movement of water within the clay itself, meaning that drying is actually occurring in two stages: first, from around the clay particles, thus bringing them into closer proximity to one another, and second, from within the network of pores formed between the particles.

Drying shrinkage occurs as the particles move closer together and is complete when they lie in contact with one another; this is known as the leather-hard stage. Clays with fine particles shrink much more than those with larger particles – so porcelain, for example, which has very fine particles and is very plastic, shrinks considerably more than other clays. Generally, wares are unlikely to crack if they survive to the leather-hard stage, but the surface of a form reaches that stage before the interior, thus creating a moisture gradient from inside to out. The faster the rate of evaporation from the surface, therefore, the greater the moisture gradient. This is the root of many problems because a big moisture gradient creates more stresses in drying, leading to warpage and cracks.

Conditions that affect drying

One might assume that making something that survives to the leather-hard stage means that the problems associated with drying have been overcome, but unfortunately there are things to consider before the wares even get to this stage – not least, the assumption that they will dry evenly. Water will evaporate from certain areas far more rapidly than others, depending on where the item is placed to dry. For instance, the bases of forms standing on boards will take much longer to dry than the walls, which have a free movement of air around them, and rims and handles will dry faster than thicker, less exposed areas of a form. This is why tiles are notoriously difficult to dry flat because the upper, exposed surface dries faster than the underside, causing it to become concave and warp.

The factors that affect drying also affect shrinkage. Placing a weight on a tile to keep it flat, for instance, will reduce shrinkage in that part of the tile. Similarly, if there are conditions causing one part of the item to dry more rapidly than the rest, acting much like an anchor, the remaining surface will have to travel towards it as it shrinks, causing uneven shrinkage, which could easily lead to warping or cracking.

Plate orientation also has a marked effect on shrinkage; see Clay Particle Orientation on page 41.

DRAUGHTS AND TEMPERATURE EXTREMES

Placing items to dry in areas exposed to draughts or direct heat (the sun, fires, even the kiln) causes uneven volume shrinkage as the softer, undried areas are compressed by the shrinkage of the dried area, creating stresses that invariably lead to cracks. It stands to reason, then, that air flow should be controlled in the drying area. The atmosphere should be ambient, preferably without extremes of either heat or cold and away from draughts.

Complete drying only takes place when the work is fired and this happens when the boiling point of water (100°C/ 212°F) is reached; thereafter, the firing process removes the chemically bound water from clay as it fires higher.

THE DRYING PROCESS IN FIRING

STAGES	TEMPERATURE	PROCESS
Initial kiln drying	100°C (212°F) Boiling point of water	Complete drying occurs. Firing must proceed slowly (50–100°C/122–212°F per hour over the first 200°C/400°F) to prevent steam pressure within the body that would lead to explosions. Bung holes remain open.
Dehydration	350–500°C (662–932°F)	Chemically combined water begins to be driven off and an irreversible chemical change occurs. There is no observable shrinkage, but from here on it is no longer possible to mix water with the dried clay to make new clay.
Burning away of organic and inorganic materials	Occurring up to 900°C (1625°F)	Carbonaceous materials contained in the clay burn away. If wares are fired too quickly between the range 600–1000°C (1112–1832°F), organic material can be sealed into the body as the surface layers vitrify; this leads to black coring and bloating in subsequent firings as pressure generated by gases from the organic material forms bubbles.
Quartz inversion	573°C (1064°F)	Quartz crystals rearrange into a different order. A slight increase in volume occurs, but is only temporary. Firing should proceed slowly through this phase.
Vitrification	Temperature dependent on clay type	Various components of the clay melt and fuse together; first the clay hardens and tightens and then partially glassifies. Shrinkage occurs as particles arrange even closer together and fuse in a glassy matrix.

Drying

Splitting seams

THE PROBLEM

Cracking at seams and joins

Component parts split along seams that have been joined together.

Applies to: Any making technique where sections are joined together.

Caused by: Joining sections at different stages of dryness; insufficient lubrication of edges to be joined; poor scoring; lack of or poor clay reinforcement to joins; wrong clay.

A thin coil of clay to reinforce the join may have helped to avoid this split.

THE SOLUTIONS

Cut all sections at the same time: Cut all sections from one slab of clay at the same time where possible – then there can be no discrepancy in stages of dryness.

Lubricate liberally: Score edges with a craft knife in a cross-hatch before applying a liberal amount of slip. Any excess can be wiped away after joining sections. Alternatively, use a stiff toothbrush and lots of water to complete both actions in one.

Reinforce joins: Where possible, reinforce joins with thin coils of soft clay; first apply a brush of slip to the seam, then press the coil along the edge, blending it in carefully. Remove any excess with a rib or kidney to give a neat finish.

Use the correct clay: Not all clays suit every making method. Toothy or grogged clay is often best for slab construction unless you are working on very small-scale wares – and even then, clay like porcelain can be very prone to splitting because there is only a small window of space when sections are at the correct stage to join.

Uneven drying

THE PROBLEM

Distortion and warping

Forms warp and crack inexplicably, despite careful making.

Applies to: Wares made by any making technique.

The rim of the bowl is clearly misshapen at the leather-hard stage – the problem will only get worse as it dries and is fired.

Caused by: Most commonly, if a form is well made with an even thickness in the clay wall and has not been distorted at the making stage, the problem is caused by drying too quickly or exposing the wares to a direct source of heat or air on one side. Uneven thickness in the clay wall can have a similar effect because thinner areas will dry faster than thicker areas, causing a tension that pulls the form out of shape.

Thick rim areas will dry much slower than thin lower sections, potentially warping the form as it dries.

THE SOLUTIONS

Dry slowly and evenly

■ Dry wares on a wooden or wire rack to allow free movement of air around the forms.
■ Dry away from direct sources of heat and out of draughts, away from open doors or windows.
■ Cover wares loosely with light plastic sheeting and allow to dry slowly.

Check even thickness of walls: Measure the thickness of clay walls with a pin occasionally when building to ensure they are even throughout the form.

Here, the form will not dry evenly because half the shape is in the sun and half is in shadow.

Drying tip

A great way to keep rims perfectly round as they dry is to place them over an upturned bowl. Cover the bowl loosely with a piece of soft plastic before inverting the form over it; this will allow for movement and shrinkage as it dries, otherwise the form may stick to the bowl and cracks will form around the rim.

Stainless steel bowls are always good shapes to use because they are perfectly round. Look out for them in charity shops.

Coiling

Initial forming

THE PROBLEM

Collapsing shape

Coiled forms begin to sag and lose shape as the form gets bigger.

Caused by: The clay is too thin to support weight as it is built up; the clay is too wet to hold the shape; wrong clay type.

THE SOLUTIONS

Return the form to the initial shape with a wooden spatula.

Reshape with a spatula: Turn the form over and paddle the base with a wooden spatula to return it to the initial shape, then dry off a little with a hairdryer.

Tighten the rim: If the rim is wider than required, cut a V-shaped section out, score and slip the surfaces of the V, then pull them together and join carefully. Smooth over with a kidney and equalize the wall thickness. Repeat around the rim if necessary.

Firm up the clay

- Use a hairdryer to firm up the clay before continuing to build. Rotate the form as you dry for an even effect.
- Firm up wet clay by wedging or kneading it on a plaster bat before rolling coils. (See Clay preparation, page 58.)

Choose the correct clay: If you are buying clay ready made, make sure it is suitable for coiling. For large or complex constructions, the best clay will generally have some grog content. Smaller forms requiring less support can usually be made from finer clay.

THE PROBLEM

Lumpy, bulging clay surface

Clay walls look uneven, bulging in places, resulting in poor shape definition.

Caused by: Poor making technique – inconsistencies in the size of coils; insufficient refining of surface, collapsing shape (see

THE SOLUTIONS

Use consistent size coils: Roll all coils to the same thickness by measuring each one against the first. Roll several at a time and keep them under soft plastic until you are ready to use them. Always reserve one to measure the next batch by.

Remove excess clay: To maintain an even wall thickness, remove excess clay from both inner and outer surfaces at regular intervals using a kidney. Do this as you progress. Always support the wall with one hand on the opposite side to prevent distorting the shape.

Measure shape and thickness of walls

- Use an outline former to keep the shape of the pot true, making corrections as described in Collapsing shape (page 74) to reshape.
- Measure the thickness of the walls at regular intervals with a pin to ensure consistency throughout the form.

Pinching

Initial shaping

THE PROBLEM

Losing control of shape

Inability to keep control of the shape at the early stage of pinching.

Caused by: Incorrect position of hands and fingers when pinching a shape. The most common outcome is that the shape flares out too quickly so that it becomes platelike.

The pinched form falls outward.

THE SOLUTIONS

Position hands correctly
■ Hold the ball of clay firmly in one hand to contain the shape.
■ Pinch the shape in stages working from the bottom of the ball, pinching in small stages up the sides towards the rim.
■ Keep the thumb or finger that is pinching from the inside crooked as you work, leaving the rim as closed as possible until you are ready to open the form out.
■ Keep practising until you get it right – observe the way you are working and make small adjustments to hand position if it continues to go wrong.
■ Refer to Best practice: pinching, page 60, for correct technique.

Use correct clay: The problem may be with the clay being used. If it is too soft, it cannot hold its shape – refer to Clay types: composition and nature, page 42, for the most suitable types of clay for pinching.

Hold clay firmly and keep thumb bent to maintain shape.

THE PROBLEM

Cracking and splitting

The clay cracks and splits as the shape is pinched.

Caused by: Most commonly, too hot hands that dry the clay out before it can be fully worked. Clay that is the wrong type and wrong consistency.

THE SOLUTIONS

Keep your hands cool: Run your hands under the cold tap from time to time to maintain an even temperature.

Keep clay moist
■ Make sure the clay is not too hard before you begin – the process of pinching dries the clay quickly because of the level of handling so it needs to be quite malleable.
■ Keep the rim moist by dabbing with a damp sponge occasionally. Don't rub the rim with the sponge; it will bring any grog in the clay to the surface and spoil the effect.
■ To minimize cracking, leave a thicker section of clay at the rim and work on this last.
■ If it becomes too difficult to work, wrap the form in a damp cloth and place in a plastic bag or box for half an hour to soften up. Don't leave too long or the shape will slump!

Use a sponge to keep rim moist.

Use correct clay: Some clays, such as porcelain, naturally dry out quickly so are harder to work with – refer to Clay types: composition and nature, page 42, for best choices.

THE PROBLEM

Uneven rims

Caused by: Pinching rims to a very fine section; uneven pinching.

Deep cracks in rims are also caused by hot hands, overworking and clay unsuitable for purpose.

THE SOLUTIONS

Pinch in small, even moves Avoid the problem by pinching the rim in small, even moves around the edge so that the correct level is maintained at all times. Don't concentrate on one area more than the rest – turn the pot continually as you work.

Level the rim

■ Place the pot on a whirler, then carefully score a line around the edge with a pin or knife, holding the hand firm as the whirler is turned. Carefully cut away the excess with a sharp knife, then smooth over the rim with a kidney to round off the edge.

■ Score the line as before but use a surform blade instead of a knife to shave away the excess. Smooth over the edge with a strip of damp chamois leather as the pot rotates on the whirler.

Make a feature of it: Many potters deliberately leave rims uneven because it gives a more organic, natural finish to the work.

Carefully cut away the excess with a sharp knife.

THE PROBLEM

Uneven shapes

The form flares outward too quickly and the shape is uneven.

Caused by: Incorrect hand position when pinching, causing the shape to flatten.

THE SOLUTIONS

Deep pinching technique: Insert thumb deeply, to a point where you can feel the pressure in the palm of the hand holding the clay. Then, keeping the thumb straight to prevent the shape being dragged to the side, gently pinch the walls to form the base shape first. Leave enough weight at the top of the form to pinch out the open shape at the end: correct the shape by paddling with a wooden spatula.

Follow the sequential diagrams for creating successful deep-pinched shapes.

Initial shaping

THE PROBLEM

Uneven shape

Caused by: Difficulty of handling as the work increases in size; clay too soft to support the weight of the form; inadvertent application of more pressure than required if it is sitting on a surface rather than being held as it is worked; lack of support at the drying stage.

This form is unbalanced and uneven.

THE SOLUTIONS

Use correct clay: Check that your clay is suitable for pinching – see Clay types: composition and nature, page 42.

Firm up consistency
■ If the clay is too wet, it will be sticky to handle. Correct by thoroughly wedging layers of wet clay and drier clay together until it is the right consistency – see Clay preparation problems, page 52.
■ If the shape begins to distort because the clay is too soft, firm it up a little with a hairdryer, taking care to dry the clay evenly.

Maintain shape: Use a template former to maintain the shape. This will also allow you to repeat the shape exactly.

Correct irregularities
■ Correct any bulges by cutting a V-shaped section from the wall at the relevant point. Cut the V diagonally so that the sections fit back together, neatly overlapping. Score and slip the V before joining back together. Repeat as required.
■ Correct small irregularities by paddling the shape with a wooden spatula. This is also a useful technique for altering the shape and smoothing the surface.

Support your work: Support larger forms by making thick clay coils for them to sit in as you work. You can also use sponges cut to shape, bowls, plaster moulds and other vessels filled with wadding, newspaper, etc. Delicate shapes should be supported as they dry to keep their shape (see below).

Using a wooden spatula can help to smooth over irregularities formed by previous handling.

Correct bulges by cutting a V-shaped section from the wall of the pot.

Ways to support forms while drying
Old dishes filled with sand, crumpled newspaper or bubble wrap (**1**). Soft coil ring – rest directly on the rim of glass jars (**2**). Bowl sitting in clay ring (**3**). Foot ring of form sitting inside the clay ring (**4**). Form sits on plastic over an upturned bowl keeping the rim rounded (**5**).

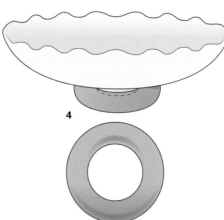

Joining

THE PROBLEM

Splits in joined pinched sections

Most problems present after biscuit firing but actually occur at the making stage.

Caused by: Poor joining; insufficient reinforcement of joins; drying too quickly; firing too quickly; uneven thickness in the clay wall; lack of air holes in work when firing.

THE SOLUTIONS

Join correctly

■ Pinch sections to be joined to exactly the same thickness – one way of doing this is to weigh the balls of clay to be pinched so they are both the same. This will give a better chance of making the sections the same size. Measure one against the other often to make sure they match.

■ The sections to be joined must be at the same level of dryness; if too wet the shapes will distort, setting up warping problems later. If too dry, a tension will be caused when the edges are wetted for joining and reinforced with soft coils. The sections should be firm but with some flexibility for shaping when joined. If one half is drier than the other, an automatic tension is set up and will result in splits.

■ If the rims to be joined are uneven, carefully shave them level with a surform blade so they fit flat together.

■ Thoroughly score and slip the joining edges, then hold the sections together for a few moments for them to fix together.

■ Make sure the join is reinforced with a coil of soft clay and blend it in well.

■ Paddling the surface gently with a wooden spatula will make sure the soft clay fills the joint.

Release moisture: It is very important to make sure you pierce a hole in the item before it dries out completely. Without a hole, trapped moisture and gases cannot escape when firing, resulting in either the work exploding completely or cracking along the join because it is the weakest point.

Dry slowly: Dry the work slowly away from draughts or excesses of heat or cold.

Use correct clay: Splits can occur because of poor clay choice – see Clay types: composition and nature, page 42, for best choice.

Fire slowly: Make sure to fire work slowly to avoid a build up of internal moisture and gases that can't escape quickly enough.

Fill crack afterwardss

If after doing all possible to avoid splits at the making stage it still happens, it may be possible to save the work by filling the crack and refiring. Pottery suppliers stock fillers for repairing biscuit-ware cracks but a simple alternative is to make a paper clay filler of your own:

1 Crush some dry clay to powder (the same clay as used to make the form).

2 Soak a few sheets of shredded toilet tissue in a small amount of white vinegar.

3 Add the dry clay to the vinegar paper little by little and mix well until the clay is firm enough to handle without being sticky.

4 Fill the crack or split with the paper clay and smooth over the surface to remove excess.

5 If you neglected to put a hole in the form first time around, make a pinhole in the newly filled split before drying and refiring.

You may need to sand the surface after firing to make it ready for its decorative treatment.

5

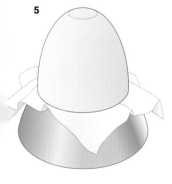

The split here is caused by poor attention to detail when making, joining or firing.

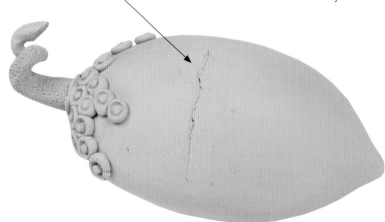

73

Throwing

Air in clay

THE PROBLEM

Air bubbles in the clay wall

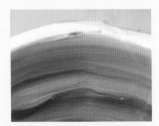

Air bubbles trapped in the clay, making it difficult to lift the walls.

Caused by: Poor preparation of clay prior to throwing; re-throwing clay after a failed first attempt.

THE SOLUTIONS

Prepare clay correctly: See Clay preparation, page 58, for correct method of de-airing clay prior to use.

Burst air bubbles: Using a potter's pin, burst the air bubbles by piercing several times. Continue to throw the form; the walls will quickly compact as you lift the wall and pinholes will seal over.

Do not re-throw: Avoid re-throwing clay; it gets tired with overuse. At the end of a throwing session, bag all used clay; reclaim or wedge it, then rest it for a few weeks.

Insert the pin deep into the bubble several times.

Collapsing forms

THE PROBLEM

Cylinder walls slump, then collapse

When pulling up the wall of the pot it suddenly begins to distort and twist, then collapses.

Caused by: Incorrect knuckling-up technique – overthinning the wall, especially at the base (undermining); throwing inconsistently, producing stresses of thicker and thinner areas in the wall – pulling the wall up too quickly; overworking the clay; using too much water; bad choice of clay (clay not fit for purpose); air bubbles in the clay (see above).

THE SOLUTIONS

Knuckle up correctly: The right forefinger should wrap around the top of the thumb; the knuckle should be placed against the outside edge of the form, with the left hand inside so that the wall is trapped between the two. Lift the clay gently and evenly from base to rim, not forgetting to neaten the rim by gently compressing the clay between finger and thumb while running a finger from the other hand over the top to smooth it.

Do not overthin walls: Overworking or knuckling up too many times will overthin the walls. Aim for a thickness of no less than 4–5 mm (⅛ in) and leave enough clay at the base to support the form as it is raised.

Do not use too much water: Avoid using an excessive amount of water; overworking tires the clay, making it weak and unable to hold its shape. Mop up excess regularly.

Use correct clay

■ Make sure your clay is a suitable type for throwing – suppliers will be able to recommend the best ones.

■ Make sure it is neither too soft nor too hard when you begin – both will create problems.

Correct knuckling up should ensure an even wall thickness.

THE PROBLEM

Collaring in collapse

The neck of the vessel being closed in to form a vase or bottle shape falls in on itself as it is narrowed. The process is called collaring in.

Caused by:

Incorrect hand position: fingers in the wrong position apply too much pressure, creating a shoulder in the form with an angle that is too extreme to hold the weight of clay above it.

THE SOLUTIONS

Collar up correctly

1 Throw a cylinder, leaving a slightly larger amount of clay on the top edge as a fat rim.
2 Mark a line in the cylinder two-thirds of the way from the base or at the point where you want the belly of the pot to end and the neck to begin; belly the form out to this point.
3 From the marked point, collar the form in by placing the left thumb over the right, with your middle fingers around the neck in a throttling action and the forefinger of your right hand over the rim inside the pot.
4 Gently bring your hands together, moving inward and upward until the required opening is achieved. A closing angle of more than 90° from the marked point will not hold shape and will naturally collapse, so keep the curve gently rounded.
5 Do not apply undue downward pressure from the finger over the rim, since $\frac{1}{8}$ in this will cause the form to collapse; you should make a lifting and closing action. Remember to lubricate your hands regularly.
6 To correct the shape if it begins to fail, gently push the wall out from the inside and in from the outside. Finish by compressing the clay at the rim as before.

Keep the shape gently rounded as the form closes in and remove the hands carefully to avoid distorting the shape.

Uneven walls and rims

THE PROBLEM

Inconsistent wall thickness

Forms are impossible to remove from the wheel head without cutting through the base: walls are thick at the base, but too thin at the rim.

Caused by: Poor throwing technique; incorrect knuckling up; overthinning the base before raising walls; misjudging the amount of clay required for the size of vessel.

THE SOLUTIONS

Check thickness: After opening up the base and before lifting the walls, measure the thickness of the clay with a pin. Push the pin through to the wheel head, then slide your fingers down until they meet the clay. Pull the pin out with your fingers still in place so that you can clearly see the thickness. If it is too thick, repeat the opening-up process.

Knuckle up correctly

■ See Collapsing forms – Cylinders (page 74) for the correct method of knuckling up. Make sure that you begin to lift the form from the base very evenly to achieve the same thickness right up to the rim.

■ Finish raising the walls using a rib instead of your knuckles or fingers; this will remove excess slurry, compact the clay, straighten the wall and smooth the surface ready for decoration. **(1)**

Getting the base thickness right

For cylinders, a base thickness of 5 mm (¼ in) is sufficient for small sizes and up to 12 mm (½ in) for larger sizes.

For forms that will be turned to form a foot ring, a greater thickness will be required; this is determined by the style of foot ring and the size of the form. It is impossible to give a definitive thickness, but it is better to allow too much than too little.

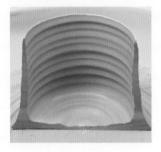

The base is clearly too thin at the centre to lift the form off the wheel successfully.

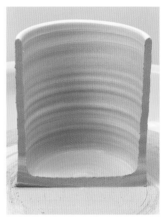

Cutaway shows correct thickness throughout the cylinder.

Once the sides of the cylinder are smooth and the wall an even thickness, decorative details can be added to create fluted lines – either horizontally or vertically. The sides can be faceted to change the shape or paddled with a wooden spatula to square the form. What is important to remember is that all these details will work far more successfully if the walls are even and the rim is level to begin with.

THE PROBLEM

Wavy, irregular rims

Rims are thin, rough and undulating or damaged.

Caused by: Inconsistent throwing; clay not being centred properly; removing your hands too quickly after throwing; not consolidating the rim after lifting.

THE SOLUTIONS

Centre clay properly: This must be done before you begin to throw. If it is even slightly out the walls will lift unevenly, causing one side of the form to be thicker than the other. This will then lead to tension in firing, causing warping and cracking.

Remove hands carefully: After lifting the walls, remove your hands gently from the rim to avoid knocking the form off-centre. If you do catch the rim, you can return it to centre by pulling up the wall one more time and then consolidating the rim.

Remove the rim

1 Hold a cutting wire taut between your fingers; then, with the wheel turning slowly, cut through the rim to a point below the damage.

2 Alternatively, use a potter's pin to perform the same task. Lift the cut section off quickly after stopping the wheel from turning.

3 Consolidate the rim again when the surplus clay has been removed.

Handle and spout problems

THE PROBLEM

Handles twist

Despite putting the handle onto a form straight, it distorts out of line in firing to look banana shaped.

Caused by: Wrong technique when pulling the handle: pulling between the forefinger and thumb in a flattening action aligns the clay particles irregularly because the clay is more compressed in the curve between finger and thumb.

Pulling the handle in the wrong way creates a banana-shaped curve to one side when fired.

THE SOLUTION

Correct technique: Once the clay has been fixed securely, pull the handle as shown so that it hangs in a downward direction. The thumb and fingers should be either side of the handle to provide equal pressure to both sides.

Handle and spout problems continued

THE PROBLEM

Teapot spout twists in firing

Teapots fail to pour properly after firing, because the spout has twisted out of position.

Caused by: This is a common problem and relates to particle alignment in the clay. When a pot is thrown, the clay is controlled or held back in the process of spinning. If the wheel turns anticlockwise, the particles in the clay align in a steep clockwise spiral from base to top. If the clay is badly twisted in the process of throwing, the principles of particle alignment will ensure that it untwists in an exaggerated way when fired. Spout twist is therefore unique to each maker and their throwing technique, but as a general guide the following answers should go some way to helping.

THE SOLUTION

Good spout making technique

1 Throw the spout as smoothly as possible, avoiding throwing marks by using the sides of fingers where possible as opposed to the tips. Make the spout longer than is required.

2 Using your little finger, tilt the tip of the spout into a gentle curve; this gives a better shape.

3 After wiring the spout off the wheel head, gently squeeze the sides at the base together as shown, in line with the direction of the spout; an ovoid shape fits much better onto a curved surface.

4 When the spout has dried to soft leather hard, cut the pouring tip on the diagonal: imagining that the opening is a clock, start at the bottom of the tip at 5 o'clock, cutting across to 11 o'clock. When the spout then shrinks in firing, it should realign to 6 o'clock.

5 Cut the body of the spout on a diagonal from the upper part of the skirt down, so that there is more clay below than above. When it is attached to the teapot body, there should now be minimal twist in firing.

THE PROBLEM

Cracks at rim and base of handles

Cracks appear at the points where the handle has been attached to the form.

Caused by: Poor joining technique; difference in dryness between the body of the form and the handle being attached; failure to score and slip the surfaces of both the form and handle butt before applying.

THE SOLUTION

Good joining technique

1 First, ensure that the form the handle is being attached to is not too dry; it should be firm enough to apply the handle without distorting the clay (leather hard, preferably).
2 When applying the rim end of the handle, join the two surfaces after scoring and slipping each beforehand. Support the inside of the form as you do so to prevent the shape from being distorted. Make sure the rim end of the handle is securely joined before pulling the handle.
3 When joining the lower end of the handle, secure it to the form with a central finger mark and then a downward sweep of the finger each side of the centre point.

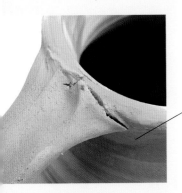

The form should not be any drier than leather hard, otherwise the handle will peel away from the form.

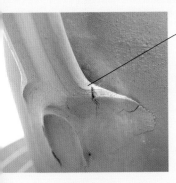

Do not spread the clay outward as shown, because the overthinning weakens the join, leading to cracks.

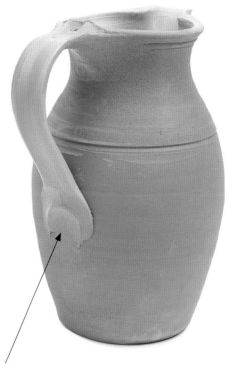

Correctly applied handle.

Cracks

THE PROBLEM

Cracks in the base of thrown forms

Cracks appear on the underside of thrown forms as they dry or more often after firing. The crack may present in an S shape or be straight.

Caused by: Not compressing the base sufficiently when throwing; failing to remove surplus water or slurry after throwing; drying wares on wheel bats; overturning the base thus creating an uneven thickness of clay wall; uneven drying.

Diagram of randomly orientated particles after failure to compress base sufficiently and after excessive turning.

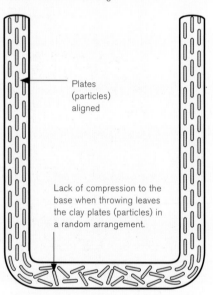

Plates (particles) aligned

Lack of compression to the base when throwing leaves the clay plates (particles) in a random arrangement.

These cracks typically occur in thrown products where the maker has not compressed the base sufficiently or failed to remove surplus water or slurry after throwing.

THE SOLUTIONS

Compress base: Compress the base of the form by running your thumb over the surface from centre to edge at least three times. You can use a knuckle rib or sponge for the last compression if you prefer. **(1)**

Remove surplus water: Remove all surplus water from the form after throwing; use a sponge for mopping internally (a sponge on a stick for deep forms, where the hand can't reach) and run a rib over the surface to remove excess slurry. Wipe excess water from the wheel head and cut a bevel around the edge of the base before wiring off. **(2)**

Remove from wheel bat: If you are throwing on wheel bats, wire the base of the form a couple of times after throwing. As soon as the form is firm enough to handle, wire it off again, then remove it to another bat in an upturned position if possible to allow the base to dry off to the same level as the body for turning. If the form does not need to be turned, it must still be removed from the bat: **never** allow a form to completely dry in situ on the bat it was thrown on.

Avoid overturning base: Ascertain the thickness of clay at the base of a form by measuring it with a pin before turning. There is no hard-and-fast preventative measure to avoid overturning a base, but practice and repetition teach when enough has been turned usually. (Even the best potters don't get this right every time!)

Dry evenly: See Drying considerations, page 66, for best practice on drying wares and Uneven drying, page 68, for solutions to drying problems.

Rim cracks

THE PROBLEM

Chittering (cracks around edges and rims)

Cracks run from the rim down the side of the pot, often from ragged edges.

Caused by: Rim section being too thin; turning the sides of a form too close to the rim; poor finishing off when throwing; drying too rapidly or unevenly; reabsorbtion of fluid (after slip application, etc.) on surfaces with uneven thicknesses.

THE SOLUTIONS

Throw even walls
- Throw even walls, avoiding thinning towards the rim.
- Never turn the sides of a form right down to the rim; this creates an uneven wall thickness and causes a ragged edge to the rim.

Consolidate rims: Consolidate rims at the end of each stage of throwing.

Dry slowly and evenly: Dry wares slowly, away from extremes of temperature or draughts, preferably on racks.

Apply slip or engobes at the leather-hard stage: If it is drier than leather hard, the absorbtion at a rim that is thinner than the body will cause it to become over-wet and set up tensions, leading to cracks in subsequent drying.

Remove rim and fill crack: As a last resort, try shaving off the ragged rim with a surform blade, then smooth over the surface with a barely damp sponge. Fill the crack with a thick paper clay slip (see Paper clays, page 51) and allow to dry. Sand the surface after biscuit firing, but be aware that the crack may reappear at higher-temperature firings.

fix-its Turning

3

Turning problems

THE PROBLEM

Losing centre

Inability to re-centre a form after knocking it out of place while turning a foot ring.

Caused by: Bad centring first time so that the position is impossible to replicate; lack of adhesion of the form to the wheel head; wrong tools; clay is in the wrong condition for turning – usually too dry.

THE SOLUTIONS

Position in the centre
1 Dampen the surface of the wheel head before beginning the centring process; this should ensure that the form stays in place once correctly positioned.
2 A pin line marking the point to turn the foot ring to will help you to gauge when the shape is centred correctly; if this is not true, the form is off-centre and needs adjustment.
3 Once the form is centred and fixed to the dampened wheel head, draw a thick pencil line around the edge to mark the position; after this, if the

form should dislodge you have an exact marker to fit it to.
Use correct tool: Instead of hard metal turning tools, choose a loop tool, as demonstrated here. Where possible, keep the fingers of your opposite hand on the form to gently hold it in place
Ensure clay is leather hard: Clay should be leather hard to turn easily; if it is drier than this, the surface will chatter or the clay will compact and almost burnish instead of cut away.

THE PROBLEM

Overturned foot ring

The foot ring is turned too thinly to support the weight of the form.

Caused by: In an attempt to refine the foot ring, too much clay is removed.

THE SOLUTION

Add a new foot ring

1 Turn the foot ring off completely, then score a position with a serrated kidney to mark the place where a new foot ring can be joined.
2 Make a doughnut of clay, apply some slip, position it on the marked area, then secure it in place with a wooden tool.

3 Throw the foot ring to the correct shape and size.

4 Turn the foot ring to the correct size again when it is firm enough.

THE PROBLEM

Chattering

Ripples in the surface of the clay are created in the process of turning the walls.

Caused by: Clay is too dry; the wrong turning tools were used; tools were blunt or insecurely held.

THE SOLUTIONS

Ensure clay is moist enough: Make sure that the clay is no firmer than leather hard. If it is drier than this and you want to try turning it anyway, run a damp sponge over the surface quickly beforehand. Alternatively, spray mist the form and seal it in a plastic bag for a while to see if it will soften the clay a little. (Don't over-wet it; the form will collapse!)

Use the correct tool:
Change the turning tool from the rigid metal type (left) to a loop tool (right); it will glide more readily over the clay.

Hold tool securely: Rest your hands firmly in place on the side of the wheel bowl when turning and use your other hand to steady and support the hand holding the tool.

A loop tool cuts through the surplus clay easily to remove excess – even when the clay is drier than optimum.

Slabbing

Uneven drying

THE PROBLEM

Warping of tiles and other flat slabs

Tiles and flat slabs curl and distort as they dry, then warp even further in firing.

Caused by: Poor making technique (slabs are of uneven thickness); incorrect drying on boards with the upper surface exposed to air or heat; poor choice of clay. See also: Uneven drying, page 68.

Tiles exposed to the air on one side only will warp as moisture is lost from the upper surface more quickly than the undersides.

THE SOLUTIONS

Dry evenly
■ Dry tiles between absorbent boards, weighting the boards to ensure that the three surfaces sandwich together properly to keep the slabs flat.

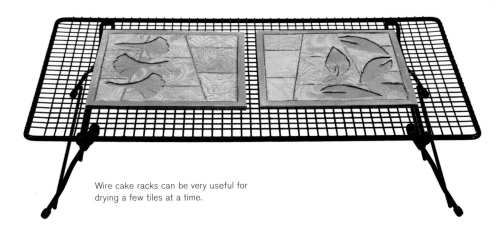

Wire cake racks can be very useful for drying a few tiles at a time.

■ Dry on wire racks to allow free movement of air. If you are working on a large scale, you will have to custom make your wire racks. Choose a sturdy wire mesh that will support the slabs to keep them flat and elevate it to allow free movement of air.
■ Once tiles are almost dry (firm leather hard) they can be stacked on their side, separated by a button or two of clay between each one and supported at each end by a kiln prop or similar, until completely dry. If this is done on a kiln shelf, the tiles can be moved directly into the kiln and fired in the same way. See also: Kiln space saving, page 134.

Ensure even thickness: If you don't have a slab roller, use wooden roller guides to ensure that the slabs are rolled to an even thickness. Turn the slabs regularly as you roll them to prevent them from sticking to the surface they are on. Rolling on plastic sheeting will ensure that the slabs don't lose moisture prematurely and make turning easier. Rolling on cotton fabric is useful if the clay is on the soft side because the fabric will absorb some of the moisture and firm the slabs a little.

Select correct clay: Grogged clay will have greater warp resistance for slab work. The coarser the grog the better – but this is not always practical where a smooth finish is required, so add 100 dust grog or fine sand in increasing small measures until you achieve a body that works for you.

Specific problems

THE PROBLEM

Slip fails to fill the mould

The mould fails to fill completely with slip, leaving empty cavities in the cast.

Caused by: Poor mould design – the pouring holes are too small, resulting in them closing up before sufficient slip has filled the cavity. This also makes it impossible to fill the mould evenly, thus causing a creasing effect as the slip thickens on contact with the plaster. Slip meet – caused when an edge of slip being poured through one opening meets slip from a second opening or if the slip does not fill the mould evenly when pouring through a single cavity. Slip meet can lead to splits and cracks. Slip is either under- or over-deflocculated.

THE SOLUTIONS

Adapt your mould: Carefully drill out larger pouring holes in the mould; this can be risky, since plaster can easily crack.

Redesign your mould:
■ Redesign the mould to have one larger opening, allowing the slip freer access.
■ Pour the slip from a point that will allow it to spread out evenly from a central point rather than to one side, where it then has to meet itself from another side as it fills.

Check deflocculation of slip
■ Check the pint weight of the slip (clay to water ratio, see page 65): the heavier the slip, the slower the run off will be. The correct weight should be available from your supplier if you are buying ready-made slip, but it is worth determining it for yourself also.
■ If the slip is under-deflocculated, add a very small amount of water or a drop or two of sodium silicate to correct the fluidity.
■ Test a pint sample of slip by adding a few drops of sodium silicate; if it thickens it has too much deflocculant.

The slip has not filled the mould fully and so cavities and creases appear.

THE PROBLEM

Wreathing

Lines form on the slip sides of casts.

Caused by: Slip developing a thin skin when it comes into contact with air, which then breaks and reforms as it is poured into or out of the mould, resulting in raised lines. Here the problem is due to uneven draining of slip, but it can also result when the thixotropy is too low or moulds are in poor condition, overly saturated or unevenly porous.

THE SOLUTIONS

Fill mould quickly and evenly: Fill the mould faster from a central point for even filling.

Drain evenly and completely
■ Rotate the mould as you empty slip after casting and drain evenly and steadily.
■ Turn upside down and wedge at a slight angle to complete draining if possible.

Check thixotropy: If thixotropy is too low, decrease the alkali addition to the slip.

Fix afterwards: Scrape away the ridges, then smooth with a damp sponge. Or, sand when the form has dried (wearing a dust mask), and sponge.

Use a natural sponge to smooth over the surface but avoid using excess water.

The effects of the slip draining unevenly can clearly be seen in these creases.

THE PROBLEM

Bad seams

Slip bleeds out at mould seams, leaving protrusions and filling areas that should be hollow (space inside the handle), leading to prominent seams after firing.

Caused by: Poor mould design; bad seam joins; mould sections not securely fixed together because of surplus clay left behind after the last casting. See Clay particle orientation, page 41.

THE SOLUTIONS

Thoughtful mould design: Design models for plaster casts so that seams can join in places where they look natural (along a coat seam in this example) but not where they might create undercuts. Careful planning of a model will overcome most casting problems. Raised seams will only appear after firing, but may be less of a problem with lower-firing slips.

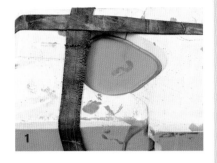

Secure mould firmly: Make sure that all the parts of the mould are held together firmly and securely with thick elastic banding. **(1)**

Clean moulds between castings: Wipe around the interior of the mould to remove any surplus specks of clay before casting again.

Fettle seams: Fettle seams very carefully to remove excess clay, using a potter's knife or fettling tool; this is best done when the form is leather hard to dry. Sponge over seams with a damp sponge to finish. **(2)**

THE PROBLEM

Lumps in the casting slip

After casting a form, lumps can be seen in the surface of the slip.

Caused by: Bits of dry slip falling back into the casting container; insufficient stirring before casting; putting slip scraps directly back into the slip.

THE SOLUTIONS

Clean thoroughly: After every casting session, clean the lid and sides of the slip bucket to remove the possibility of slip drying out and falling back in.

Stir thoroughly: Stir slip thoroughly for several minutes before casting and remove any lumps detected if possible.

Sieve: Pour the slip through a sieve to catch any lumps. **(1)**

Reclaim in small amounts: Dried scraps of slip should never be put back into the mixture because they remain lumpy, thus causing the problem seen. It is better to collect scraps over time then reclaim it in one batch, but because you cannot know the amount of deflocculant in the reclaim mix it can only be added in small amounts to a new batch in order not to upset the balance. It can therefore all be used again but only over time as new batches of slip are produced.

CHAPTER 4 SURFACE

DECORATION

FOR MANY PEOPLE STARTING OUT IN POTTERY, SURFACE
DECORATION IS AN AFTERTHOUGHT – AND THE AREA WITH
THE GREATEST POTENTIAL PITFALLS. THE BIG PROBLEM LIES
IN THE FACT THAT FAULTS OCCUR AFTER FIRING AND
THEREFORE A STAGE BEYOND WHICH THE ITEM CAN
USUALLY BE SAVED. THIS CHAPTER LOOKS AT SOME OF THE
MOST WIDELY ENCOUNTERED ISSUES, OFFERING IDEAS FOR
BEST PRACTICE TO AVOID THE FAULTS WHERE POSSIBLE
AND FIX-ITS FOR WHEN THE WORST HAPPENS.

Surface decoration

Many problems arising in relation to surface decoration of greenware and biscuit ware are associated with slips and engobes (an engobe is a slip containing an amount of flux to fire it onto a biscuit surface as opposed to a greenware surface). It is obvious that applying a liquid clay to a drier clay surface could lead to faults, but understanding certain fundamental principles will not only help you avoid such faults, but will also form a good basis for experimentation.

Slip basics

- If applied thinly enough, most clay slips will fit most clay bodies; but if a thicker coat is required, the slip should match the clay body for shrinkage purposes.
- Given that slip is wetter than the surface it is applied to and therefore has more to shrink, the slip recipe should have lower drying shrinkage than the clay body.
- If the slip covering shrinks more or less than the body it is covering, then it will flake or crack as it dries. Some potters make use of this fault as a form of surface decoration in its own right, but for most purposes it is important to avoid such stresses.
- Variations in the viscosity of the slip can lead to inconsistencies in shrinkage, so it is important to keep a check on this and correct periodically.
- Apply slip to surfaces when the clay is as wet as possible (but handleable) for best fit and to avoid shrinkage variations.
- A good way of matching slip to body is to use the same clay. This is most practicable for white firing clays, which can be refined by sieving to remove grog or molochite and then coloured with oxides or body stains.

◄ TONY LAVERICK
This thrown and turned bowl will have been fired at least three times at different temperatures using glazes, slips, engobes, chlorides and oxides.

Methods of slip application

SPONGING

This is a great way of applying multicoloured layers of slip to give a surface depth and subtle texture. It is also useful when working with resists such as paper, wax or latex. Shaped sponges can also be used to apply specific patterns and designs onto surfaces.

Use a fine, natural sponge for applying background colours of slip and synthetic sponges for design shapes. An easy way of making a shaped sponge is to soak it in water, squeeze most of the water out then freeze the sponge before cutting it to shape.

◄ Lightly sponge the colour around the edges of the paper shapes, leaving areas exposed to see where they can be lifted off later.

DIPPING

Make sure the slip is deep enough to immerse the form into and that the container is large enough to avoid the form touching either the bottom or sides. Like pouring, dipping is a good way of applying an even coat of slip – but again it is important to consider how the form will be held for the process. Forms thrown on bats can be dipped while still in situ, then wired off after to avoid having to handle them. Repair finger marks quickly while the slip is still fluid to allow the mark to heal over and to avoid a permanent scar.

▲ A spray booth allows for great experimentation with slips and glazes because they can be applied in subtle layers.

SPRAYING

This is a useful method when pouring or dipping is too difficult because of the size or shape of the piece, when you have too little slip for other application methods or you want to achieve a subtle design effect. Note that:

- The slip should not be too thick for this method – otherwise it will block the spray gun.
- The form being sprayed should be on the dry side of leather hard to absorb the thinner-than-usual slip.
- Spraying should not continue for too long, otherwise runs will form.
- It is better to build up the surface gradually, allowing each layer to dry off a little before you apply the next coat.

There are many other decorative ways of using slip – marbling, feathering, slip trailing, spotting and so on – but almost all of the problems that may arise will ultimately relate to clay fit and shrinkage, so by following these principles of best practice, it should be possible to avoid them for the most part.

POURING

This method gives a good, even coating of slip, but wares should be easy to hold for ease of application. Foot rings are useful because they allow a form to be rotated easily as the

◄ Support the form by holding it with a spread hand on the inside and dip up to the rim in a quick action to avoid over-saturation.

◄ Pouring is a simple method of applying slip evenly and is a method used often by potters using rustic techniques.

89

Glazing

There is nothing more disappointing than opening a kiln to find that your glazing has failed. Occasionally the problem arises from defects in the glaze, but it is more likely to result from a lack of understanding of the glaze itself and how the constituent parts work together in the recipe. It may also be the result of poor application or incorrect firing. There is plenty of information available via books and the Internet to show how to apply glaze, so this section will concentrate more on the glaze itself and on the firing process.

▲ PIPPIN DRYSDALE
This piece comes from the series 'Tanami Mapping' and involves a complex layering of various different glazes.

The purpose of glazing

In simple terms, a glaze is a mixture of compounds that, when applied to the surface of clay and fired in a kiln, melt into a kind of glass. At a basic level, the purpose of glazing a surface is purely practical: for instance, functional wares are glazed to make them water-resistant and easy to clean, but the glaze also makes the wares more durable. At a creative level, glazing offers makers enormous scope to develop their own unique surface signature because it is so versatile: it can, for instance, be shiny, satin or matt; it can offer a wonderfully rich palette of colours or be muted and just as delicious in a quiet understated way; it can be textured and volcanic or crazed in appearance; or it can used in layers to build up sophisticated patterns and designs.

FLUXES: THEIR SOURCES AND OTHER USEFUL INFORMATION

The following basic oxides are the most commonly used active fluxes in glaze formulation.

FLUX BASIC OXIDES	SOURCE	TEMPERATURE/ FIRING RANGE		SOLUBLE	THERMAL EXPANSION	POISONOUS
		Minimum	Maximum			
Lead oxide	Litharge Galena Red lead White lead (lead carbonate) Lead monosilicate Lead bisilicate Lead sesquisilicate	800°C (1472°F)	1180°C (2156°F)	Slightly	Low	Yes Safe fritted leads used in low-solubility glazes
Boric oxide	Colemanite Borax Boracite (Found in combination) Boric acid	800°C (1472°F)	1400°C (2552°F)	Yes	Very low	No
Sodium oxide	Feldspars China stone Nepheline syenite Borax Cryolite (Found in combination) Sodium carbonate Sodium bicarbonate Also wood ash	850°C (1562°F)	1400°C (2552°F)	Yes	High	No
Potassium oxide	Feldspar China stone Nepheline syenite (Found in chemical combination) Potassium carbonate (pearl ash) Potassium nitrate	900°C (1652°F)	1400°C (2552°F)	Yes	High	No
Zinc oxide	Zinc oxide	1050°C (1922°F)	1400°C (2552°F)	No	Low	Yes
Calcium oxide	Feldspar Dolomite China stone Nepheline syenite Colemanite Calcium sulphate Wollastonite Bone ash (calcium phosphate) Fluorspar (Found in combination) Calcium carbonate (chalk, limestone, marble)	1100°C (2012°F)	1400°C (2552°F)	No	Medium	No
Barium oxide	Barium sulphate (barytes) Barium carbonate	1150°C (2102°F)	1400°C (2552°F)	No	Medium	Yes
Magnesium oxide	Dolomite Talc Boracite China stone (Found in combination) Magnesium carbonate	1150°C (2102°F)	1400°C (2552°F)	No	Very low	No

GENERAL GUIDELINES

■ **Use more water than less;** any excess can be siphoned off with a sponge once the glaze has settled.

■ **If you want to maintain conformity** in consistency of glaze from batch to batch, use a glaze hydrometer.

■ **The ratio of glaze to water** is generally dependant on the porosity of the wares to be covered, especially when dipping, but this is something best measured by trial and error because so much will depend on the requirements of the maker. As a rule, however, the glaze should be thicker for relatively vitreous items and quite dilute for porous biscuit.

■ **Transparent glazes** need only be applied thinly.

■ **Matt, coloured or white glazes** benefit from a thicker application.

■ **Stoneware glazes** can be applied more thickly than earthenware.

■ **If you have a limited** amount of glaze, cover large items first.

■ **Always mix glaze** thoroughly before each use – and periodically if you are glazing over a long period of time.

■ **Clean the lid** and sides of the glaze bucket after use to prevent glaze drying out and falling back into the slop – to avoid problems when glazing next time.

■ **Avoid storing glaze** in metal containers; it will cause the glaze to settle out more quickly.

■ **Always test glazes** before they are used to cover a whole body of work. Also test mixes when new batches are prepared because raw materials can vary greatly according to where they were sourced and how they have been processed.

Glaze composition

There are three essential ingredients in glaze: silica or silicon dioxide (the glass-forming element); flux such as zinc oxide or calcium oxide, which controls the melting of the glaze; and alumina or aluminium dioxide, which provides stability and helps to bind the glaze to the clay body. Many ingredients may be combined to make a glaze, but these three separate parts must be present.

In simple terms, a glaze is a combination of one or more basic oxides (fluxes), plus an acid oxide (silica) and a neutral oxide (alumina) to balance the mix.

FLUX

The most important ingredient is the flux because this forms the base of the glaze and determines the temperature at which the glaze will melt as well as its colour and texture. The flux acts as a solvent for the silica (acid oxide) when the various components of the glaze become chemically active during firing.

As a general rule, the greater the amount of alumina and silica in a glaze, the higher the firing temperature will need to be. Alumina and silica are sourced from clay minerals and flint; fluxes are sourced from a variety of minerals.

PROPORTION OF ACID AND NEUTRAL OXIDES TO FLUX

Acid oxides include silica, which can be in the form of quartz; flint; sand; feldspar; china clay, or china stone; and boric oxide (borax, which is fritted soda and oxide).

When developing glazes it is vital to get the proportions of acid oxide to flux and acid oxide to neutral oxide correct. Usually, one measure of flux is used to 2–4 measures of acid oxide. Soft glazes, for example, require one measure of flux to

Mixing glaze

Once glaze ingredients are mixed together with water, the mix is referred to as slop glaze. When mixing a glaze, wear a dust mask to avoid breathing in potentially poisonous materials.

1 Weigh individual ingredients carefully and accurately.

2 Put the ingredients into a bowl or bucket.

2–3 measures of acid oxide; hard glazes require one measure of flux to 3–4 measures of acid oxide.

The proportion of neutral oxide (alumina) to acid oxide (silica) is between one-fifth and one-tenth. These examples demonstrate the proportions involved.

Example 1 Flux   = 100 g (100 oz)*
                     (1 measure)
        Acid oxide   = 200 g (200 oz)
                     (2 measures)
        Neutral/Alumina = 10–20 g (10–20 oz)

Example 2 Flux   = 100 g (100 oz)
        Acid oxide   = 400 g (400 oz)
        Neutral/Alumina = 40–80 g (40–80 oz)

*These are not direct conversions. Please choose either the metric or imperial measurement.

The choice of flux is important, since this determines the melting and fusing point of the glaze. Base fluxes are usually used in combination in glaze formulation – but however many are used, they must always amount to a total of one.

Frits

Frits are compounds commonly used in glazes as fluxes that mature, i.e. they reach their optimum melting point to bond with the clay body without blemishing, below 1150°C (2102°F). The process involves melting together glaze materials (which are generally soluble in water and stomach acid and/or are toxic), then milling or regrinding them to produce a combination that is insoluble.

Most ready-made glazes in powder or slop form are now classified as either low-solubility or leadless. Low-solubility glazes contain lead, but in a fritted form, which makes them safe to use.

The following frits are the most widely used:

FRIT	TYPE	FIRING RANGE
Lead bisilicate frit	Low solubility	880–1050°C (1616–1922°F)
Lead sesquisilicate	Low solubility	860–1040°C (1580–1904°F)
Standard borax	Leadless	900–1050°C (1652–1922°F)
Soft borax (slightly alkaline; gives turquoise with copper)	Leadless	900–1050°C (1651–1922°F)
High-temperature borax (suitable for mid-temperature and stoneware glazes)	Leadless	1030–1180°C (1886–2156°F)
Ferro crystal frit (very low alumina frit used in crystalline glazes)	Leadless	1000–1100°C (1832–2012°F)
Calcium borate (used as a substitute for colemanite)	Leadless	1030–1180°C (1886–2156°F)
White zircon borax	Leadless	960–1160°C (1760–2120°F)
High alkali frit	Leadless	860–1060°C (1580–1940°F)
Low expansion frit (used for resistance to crazing)	Leadless	1020–1150°C (1868–2102°F)

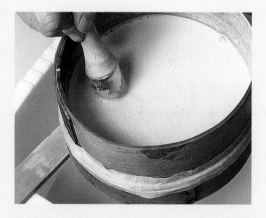

3 Cover with water and mix.

4 Sieve through an 80-mesh lawn sieve.

5 Mix colouring pigments separately with water and sieve through a 120- or 200-mesh cup lawn sieve before adding to the slop glaze.

6 Sieve again through an 80-mesh lawn sieve.

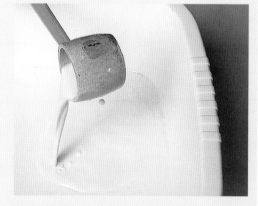

7 Leave glaze to settle overnight. It should be the consistency of double cream.

The glaze firing

As glaze is fired, it softens so that, with increasing temperature, it fuses and melts. Once the glaze fires above the biscuit temperature, the clay body becomes active again and gases are driven off which then have to escape through the glaze layer. The gases form bubbles as the glaze melts, which burst as they reach the surface, causing craters or pinhole-type marks. To allow the bubbles to settle out and dissipate, it is usual to 'soak' (hold at the top temperature) the glaze for anything from 10 minutes to half an hour or longer, to allow the glaze to flow and the marks to heal over.

▼ NATASHA DAINTRY
'Ocean' is made up of 1000 slip-cast porcelain tubes glazed in myriad colours.

Understanding silica inversions

Silica is the decomposition product of volcanic rocks and is found abundantly in clays, sandstones and flint. All ceramic clays contain this material, either combined with the clay mineral, freely (uncombined) or added in calcined form (ground flint pebbles or silica sand). Crystals of silica are subject to changes in shape and volume at certain temperatures. Some of these changes are permanent and referred to as **conversions**; others, known as **inversions**, are reversible.

SILICA CHANGES ON HEATING

573°C (1063°F) ⟶
Free silica inverts from alpha to beta quartz and expands by 1 per cent.
870°C (1598°F) ⟶
Beta quartz starts to convert to beta cristobalite and beta tridymite, which occupy 16 per cent more volume than quartz.

SILICA CHANGES ON COOLING

870°C (1598°F) ⟶
Conversion to cristobalite and tridymite ends.
573°C (1063°F) ⟶
Beta quartz inverts to alpha quartz and contracts by 1 per cent.
225°C (439°F) ⟶
Beta cristobalite inverts to alpha cristobalite and contracts by 3 per cent.
163°C (325°F) ⟶
Beta tridymite inverts to alpha tridymite and contracts by 1 per cent.

The formation of cristobalite happens in high firing; it happens slowly and is mainly affected by firing time. The greater the amount of cristobalite formed, the greater the thermal expansion and contraction, resulting in greater craze resistance of glaze.

The conversion of beta quartz to cristobalite begins above 1000°C (1832°F) and increases rapidly above 1200°C (2192°F). Because earthenware bodies are not fired as highly as stoneware bodies, they generally have a higher free silica content to enable sufficient conversion to produce enough cristobalite. Stoneware bodies go through a longer and higher heating phase, so less free silica is required and there is better integration of body to glaze, making crazing less likely.

THE CHANGES THAT TAKE PLACE IN GLAZE FIRING

Clay types are generally fired within a range of temperatures depending on the body, but all firings proceed in the same way despite the final temperature reached. This chart shows the various stages the glaze firing proceeds through, clearly showing what is happening at critical points as temperature rises and cools.

TEMPERATURE	WHAT IS HAPPENING
20–200°C (36–392°F)	■ The bungs should be open. ■ Any remaining pore water is evaporated from the clay body. ■ Firing should proceed slowly to avoid cracking or crazing.
200–500°C (392–932°F)	■ The bungs should still be open. ■ Speed of firing can be increased.
470–700°C (878–1292°F)	■ The bungs can be closed. ■ Quartz inversion occurs at 573°C (1063°F). ■ Chemically combined water is mostly driven off. ■ Carbonates begin disassociation. ■ Temperature must continue to rise slowly for once-fired wares; glaze can crawl if it is fired too quickly.
650–1000°C (1202–1823°F)	■ Glaze sinters (powdery glaze materials fuse together – the stage reached before melting). ■ Carbon burns away. ■ Continue to fire once-fired items very slowly to avoid bloating.
880–1100°C (1616–2012°F)	■ The bungs should remain closed. ■ Body shrinkage begins. ■ Sulphates in the body decompose and are driven out.
1030–1170°C (2196–2138°F)	■ Depending on the glaze type, the clay body and glaze seal together. ■ Mullite formation begins (alkalis in the clay acting upon the silica and alumina form a network of crystals known as mullite and glass, which binds the undissolved material into a strong mass). ■ The fired strength of the clay increases quickly.
1100°C (2012°F) – top temperature	■ The glaze should be soaked to allow bubbles to dissipate and the glaze to smooth over – or the firing rate should be slowed for the same reason. ■ Gases escape through unglazed areas if the interface between glaze and body has sealed. ■ The body continues to shrink and vitrify. ■ If items have been badly made or are not sufficiently supported, they can distort at this stage.
1100–750°C (2012–1382°F)	■ The molten glaze begins to cool. ■ Transparent glazes should be cooled quickly for optimum transparency, but some glazes may need controlled cooling for special effects (crystalline glazes for instance or zircon opacified glazes).
750–600°C (1382–1112°F)	■ The bungs should remain closed. ■ Cooling must be slower now, so that the temperature is uniform throughout the kiln as the point of quartz inversion moves closer. ■ The glaze hardens at this stage and begins to be compressed by the body as it cools.
600–500°C (1112–932°F)	■ The bungs should remain closed. ■ Quartz inversion is reached at 573°C (1063°F). ■ Cooling should be slow to avoid dunting at this stage.
500–150°C (932–302°F)	■ The bungs should remain in until the temperature is below 200°C (392°F) – preferably lower. ■ Cristobalite inversion occurs at 225°C (437°F), so cooling should be slow at this stage if the body contains this material.

Colour and opacity in glazes

Glazing is a complete subject in its own right and many makers spend years experimenting with ingredients and colour to produce a finish unique to them. There are many books on the market to help explore the exciting possibilities of glazes and some are recommended at the end of the book, but this section should help you to understand what is happening when glaze is coloured or opacified, so that you can quickly identify and overcome any problems that arise.

Colouring

Glazes can be coloured with either metallic oxides or glaze/body stains, which are commercially prepared pigments. In a transparent glaze these colour additions will still allow the clay body to show through when fired and wonderful effects can be achieved – especially where the colour pools in recesses and texture on the clay surface.

Opacity

Opaque glazes cover the clay body so that it does not show through. Opacity is created by the presence of crystals, air bubbles, undissolved particles or a different refractive element, and occurs because of light reflection and refraction.

Tin or zircon are most commonly used to opacify a glaze. Titanium dioxide is also used, although it lends a creamy tint to the glaze and has a matting effect. Zinc oxide and dolomite are regularly used to make matt white glazes.

Opaque matt glazes are dependent on the thickness of application and there being sufficient time in firing for the crystals to develop properly; any deviation from these principles will lead to a reduction in opacity and the glaze becoming shiny.

▲ FRANÇOIS RUEGG
This slip-cast porcelain form uses a platinum lustre and transparent glaze on the exterior and sprayed colour pigment and frit on the inside.

▶ MIKE LALONE
The ash glaze on this piece has been fired to cone 6 in oxidation, which results in a beautiful 'crawled'-looking surface.

COLOUR ADDITIONS

The chart below shows what colour response you can expect when adding these oxides to a glaze in the recommended amounts. Colour response can be affected by other ingredients in a glaze mix, so testing is always recommended first.

OXIDE	% ADDITION TO GLAZE	COLOUR RESPONSE
Antimony oxide (Toxic)	2–10	Yellow when added to high lead glaze
	7–17	White
Black cobalt oxide (Toxic)	0.1–2	Deep blue; black in higher amounts Inky blue in lead glaze Brilliant blue in alkaline glaze Purple-blue in high-firing magnesia glazes
Cobalt carbonate (Toxic)	0.1–2	Blues – as per black cobalt
Chromium oxide (Toxic)	0.5–2	Opaque green Red/orange in low-fire lead glaze Khaki, yellow, brown in the presence of zinc Incorporation of tin produces pink (chrome tin pink)
Copper carbonate (Toxic)	0.5–4	Red in reduction Green in lead glaze Note: Copper compounds should not be added to low-solubility glaze for domestic wares; it can be added to leadless glazes
	3–7	Gives a more even colour response; there is less specking than with the copper oxide
Copper oxide (Toxic)	0.5–5	Greens Turquoise in alkaline glazes Reds in reduction Note: Copper is a strong flux at all temperatures; can make glazes very runny.
Crocus martis (purple iron)	1–5	Mottled browns and yellows in stoneware glazes
Iron oxide – red iron	1–7	Honey yellows to dark brown in lead glazes Shades of green in stoneware glazes containing feldspar and whiting and fired in reduction
Yellow ochre iron	3–8	Yellows to light brown
	5–8	Brown tending to red
Magnetic iron Black iron	10 +	Black where thickly applied; red and brown on edges
Ilmenite	1–7	Combined form of iron and titanium oxides used to create brown speckling in glaze
Manganese carbonate	1–5	Pinks to brown
Manganese dioxide	0.5–8	Pinks to brown, but stronger than manganese carbonate
Nickel oxide	1–3	Brown or green; most commonly used to modify other colours In stoneware glazes containing zinc, yellow in oxidation, purple or blue in reduction
Nickel dioxide (Toxic)	1–3	Ice blue, yellow, muted greens
Potassium bichromate	1–10	Red/orange in high lead glazes fired below 1000°C (1832°F)
Rutile	2–10	A form of titanium and iron used to produce speckling Buff, brown, deep blue-grey
Tin	2–8	Up to 8% will opacify a glaze, producing a white finish; more will make most glazes crawl Pinks when combined with chrome
Titanium dioxide	5–10	Will opacify a glaze; slightly matt; cream colour May be used to supply seed crystals in crystalline glazes
Vanadium (Toxic)	5–10	Yellows in glazes containing tin
Zirconium	6–15	White; opaque Used in place of tin in glazes containing chrome to produce pale greens

Note: Certain oxides are volatile when being fired and can seriously affect other wares in the kiln. Copper is renowned for this, so to avoid problems of this nature, it is advised to fire glaze types together; if this is not possible, separate types on different levels in the kiln.

Slip and engobe faults

Problems associated with slips and engobes usually relate to a decorating technique and can therefore be rectified before the item is fired. Where a fault only becomes apparent after glaze firing, little can be done to remedy it – but understanding why it has occurred will help you to prevent it from happening again.

Post-firing problems

THE PROBLEM

Flaking after firing

Slip flakes or shears away from the surface – most notably around the rim of wares and usually only after a glost firing (glaze firing).

Caused by: A difference in firing shrinkage between the slip and clay body, exacerbated by the compressive action of the glaze in firing. Flaking is most common on convex surfaces, rims or edges and often where ball or china clay slips are applied to red earthenware bodies.

THE SOLUTION

Add flux to the slip: Test by adding 20 per cent of glaze to the slip mixture to increase the fired shrinkage. The glaze acts like a glue, improving the reaction layer between the slip and body surface and thus bonding them together better.

Change the slip recipe: Reduce the quantity of low-fired shrinkage materials such as quartz, flint, china clay or others, and replace with feldspar, Cornish stone, nepheline syenite, or other fluxes. See page 91 for a list of common fluxes.

■ If either of the above solutions makes the problem worse, add alumina, quartz or china clay to the slip and reduce or remove the flux content.

Rescue options: If you feel the work is worth trying to save, apply a little glaze over the sheared areas and refire, then disguise with an enamel colour or lustre, firing it on to the appropriate temperature.

Flaking typically shows on the rim of the bowl.

Using paper resist

THE PROBLEM

Slip bleed under paper resist

Slip bleeds or seeps underneath the paper shapes forming the decoration, blurring the crispness of the outline.

Caused by: Poor application technique; paper not being wet enough to stick; slip being too thin and watery.

THE SOLUTION

Preventing seepage method:

1 Have all the shapes for the design cut out and ready to apply in one go – plus a bowl of water. Newspaper works best, because it quickly absorbs water. Dip the paper shapes in water, then place in position on leather-hard clay. Brush the paper shape from the centre outward with a damp brush; this will displace any trapped water and seal it to the surface.

2 Apply slip that is at least the consistency of single cream and preferably a little thicker. In the same way as applying the paper design, brush the slip from the edge of the paper design outward, leaving the centre uncovered so that you can see where it is to remove later.

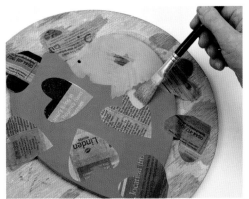

3 Alternatively, sponge the slip on using a fine natural sponge with a close texture for even coverage.

The slip is too liquid and has subsequently leaked underneath the resist, causing blurred edges.

4 Remove the paper carefully, using a pin or sharp knife to lift at an edge.

Touching up: Slip that has bled under the paper can sometimes be scraped away carefully with a sharp blade and touched up with a fine brush and a little slip. Alternatively, try drawing a sgraffito design over the messy areas to define the outline.

Successful sgraffito

THE PROBLEM

Sgraffito: Messy line definition

In the process of drawing in the sgraffito design, the clay burrs, leaving messy line definition.

Caused by: Working at the wrong stage of dryness; poor technique.

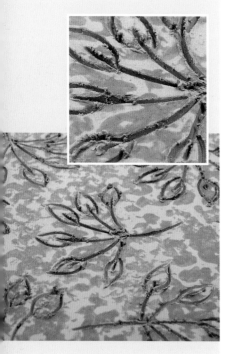

Sgraffito shows burrs where the design has been badly drawn into the surface.

THE SOLUTIONS

Removing burrs: Allow the form to dry, then remove the burrs with a fine brush. After biscuit firing it is also possible to give the surface a very fine sanding to remove any sharp burrs left behind; make sure there is no dust left on the surface before applying glaze.

Creating defined sgraffito: Draw your design first on tracing paper cut to the exact outline of the form. It is easy in this example because the shape is flat, but for three-dimensional items you will need to transcribe each part of the design individually. Draw through the design so that the outline is scored into the clay.

Best tools for the job: Use a pin and, rather than holding it upright and dragging it through the clay, draw it through gently at as flat an angle as possible.

■ Use a narrow-ended loop tool to sgraffito the lines; they will be slightly wider but much better defined, with little or no burring.

Working with inlay

THE PROBLEM

Sgraffito: Difficulty with inlay pattern

Slip is hard to remove after inlaying sgraffito lines, causing the surrounding clay to become smudged and look messy.

Caused by: Scraping the slip away before it is sufficiently dry; clay being too wet.

THE SOLUTION

Clay suitability
- Make sure that the clay body is leather hard before applying inlay.
- Make the slip from the same clay as the body to ensure a good fit. If your clay is grogged, put it through a fine mesh sieve first to refine it, then colour it accordingly.

Inlay technique

1 Use very thick slip for inlay if possible and apply it just in the lines rather than all over the surface.

2 Wait until the surface is almost but not quite dry before scraping away the excess clay. Use a metal kidney and work on small areas, following the lines of the pattern. **(1)**

3 Carefully dispose of the slip scraped away to avoid possible cross contamination into other bodies.

Dry the form completely: Remove the excess slip by sanding away with fine sandpaper. You must wear a dust mask to do this and it requires careful handling of the form because it is at its most vulnerable at this stage. **(2)**

1

2

Mastering burnishing

THE PROBLEM

Poor burnishing

Marks are created on the clay surface when burnishing, spoiling the desired smooth and polished-looking finish.

Caused by: Burnishing at the wrong stage; poor burnishing technique; wrong burnishing tools.

Using the tip of the stone creates ridges and unsightly marks.

THE SOLUTION

Burnish when leather hard: If the surface is any softer, the clay or slip will be sticky and deeper marks will be made, which will be hard to get rid of.

Hands free: Avoid touching the clay with your bare hands – wear a cotton glove to hold the form. Finger marks always remain.

Increase surface contact: Whether using a burnishing stone, spoon or other tool, always work it with as much of the flat side contacting the surface as possible.

Method 1 Burnish first with a stone or back of a flat spoon, then dry the surface off a little with a hairdryer, and repeat with the stone or spoon.

2 Using a Lucy tool (a double-ended plastic tool usually used for plaster work), burnish over the surface in one direction from top to bottom, then back again in a rapid action. **(1)**

1

2

3 Run the hairdryer over the surface again, then finely smooth using a plastic rib, holding it at a very flat angle to remove any remaining surface marks. Complete by buffing with a wad of cotton wool. **(2)**

Never fire above 960°C (1760°F): This will fire out the burnish and the form will lose its shine. Surface marks will also be more marked if the item is fired higher. Finish with a coating of polish to maximize the look and feel of the burnish.

Working with engobe

THE PROBLEM

Blurred pattern when using engobe as inlay on a biscuit body

When wiping back, the pattern becomes blurred and indistinct in certain areas.

Caused by: Using sponges and too much water to wash away excess engobe; texture to be inlaid is not sufficiently defined to contain the engobe.

Too much water has been used here and so the inlay has become blurred.

THE SOLUTION

Texture depth: Make sure that the surface to be inlaid is deeply textured so that it will contain enough engobe when the surface is wiped back with a sponge. Old lace, crochet lace, blown vinyl wallpaper and old printing blocks all make good, deep patterns in the clay surface and are perfect for this type of treatment.

Sanding engobe
1 Apply a really thick coat of engobe to the biscuit surface to completely fill the texture. Sometimes you may need to apply two or more coats for best effect. Allow to dry completely.

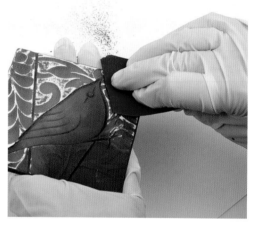

2 Wearing latex or rubber gloves and, most importantly, a dust mask, remove the top layer of engobe with fine sandpaper. Work over a sheet of paper to contain the dust as it is removed and carefully brush away any excess from the surface. This will give a much more clearly defined pattern than washing, but subtle variations can be achieved by combining both techniques if required.

Glaze faults

Glazing is fraught with problems; just a few degrees of difference in the firing temperature can have a devastating effect. This is less of a problem if the item is under-fired, because it can be fired again – but if it is over-fired, the surface will be ruined. It is key to understand what is happening when a surface is glazed so that, if things do go wrong, you can make adjustments. See Best practice: Glazing, page 90.

Poorly fired glaze

THE PROBLEM

Blistering

The surface of the glaze looks as if bubbles have burst but not sealed over properly. In severe cases the entire surface may be covered with what looks like a boiled liquid that has frozen in place.

Caused by: Over-firing: firing temperature too high; rapid firing; insufficient soaking; rapid initial cooling; wares placed too close to the elements of the kiln showing blistering on one side only; in gas- or oil-fired kilns, the problem can occur where wares are directly in the flame path (flame flashed); sometimes oxides or stains (especially manganese) can release gases during firing, which can cause blistering; excess amounts of whiting in a glaze; overuse of underglaze medium in the application of colour decoration.

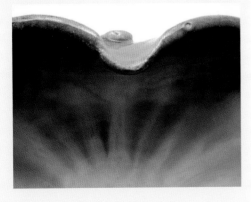

Popped bubbles blister the rim of this piece.

THE SOLUTION

Check your kiln: Is it working properly? Are the elements healthy? Is the programmer working correctly? Check also that you programmed in the correct firing cycle; it is very easy to leave the kiln set to the last firing cycle you used.

Firing accurately: Do not fire to a higher temperature or for longer than recommended for your glaze. Not only will this cause over-firing and blistering, but you run the risk of the glaze running off onto the kiln shelves and ruining them. See the chart on page 117 for recommended firing cycles.

Look at the position of the wares in the kiln: If blistering only occurs in items next to elements but not when they are placed in a central position, make a note not to position things too close next time. Understand your kiln (most have hot and cold spots) and use the knowledge to your advantage when placing items.

Slow it down: Rapid firing as glaze and body reach maturity can cause problems, especially in small, low-thermal-mass kilns, which also tend to cool down rapidly; this has the effect of freezing the bubbles in the glaze. Try slowing down the temperature rise as the glaze reaches its top temperature and/or soaking for a short time. Or try firing the temperature down over the first 50–100°C (122–212°F) from the top temperature to allow the bubble to melt.

Lower the fired viscosity of the glaze: Try replacing some feldspar or nepheline syenite with borax frit. Be aware that zircon glazes can be very viscous, so try partially replacing them with tin oxide.

Avoid gas bubbles
■ Use coloured stains as opposed to oxides where possible; these are made from calcined or fritted oxides and carbonates and are largely inert, so produce fewer gases.
■ Be conscious of glaze materials that are more gaseous. Whiting and dolomite are inclined to produce large amounts of carbon dioxide and extensive bubbling. Try using wollastonite (calcium silicate) to introduce calcium into a glaze where required; it produces far less gas.
■ Where underglaze medium has been used, it is essential not to fire the wares too rapidly. Slow down the firing to give the gases produced time to dispel and the bubbles melt out.

Lumps and bulges

THE PROBLEM

Bloating

Bulges appear in the clay wall after firing the clay to maturity. The bulges can look like small blisters in the clay or larger swellings that are hollow when broken open.

Caused by: Gases trapped in the clay when firing to vitrification (the problem is therefore most common in stoneware and porcelain bodies); over-firing; firing too quickly; the clay body containing volatile materials such as manganese dioxide, copper or iron ochre.

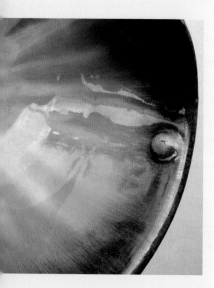

The bloat can be clearly seen as a large, but unburst, bubble in the clay.

THE SOLUTIONS

■ Many of the solutions for blistering also apply to bloating (see page 103).

Identifying the bloat: Over-firing bloats tend to be smaller and concentrated at the surface, while trapped carbon bloats are usually larger and occur at the centre of the item. If a firing contains glazed and unglazed items made from the same clay and only the glazed items bloat, the problem would appear to be trapped gases being prevented from escaping by the glaze layer rather than over-firing.

Lower the temperature: Lower the top firing temperature by 20°C (68°F) when next firing.

Change your glaze recipe: To work with the lower temperature replace potash feldspar with a vigorous flux such as soda feldspar, nepheline syenite or borax frit, so that it will mature at the same temperature.

Clay constitution

■ When sourcing and processing your own clay, test each new batch before committing work to it. A small difference in the source material can make a devastating difference.

■ Make the clay body more refractory by adding china clay, fire clay or a refractory ball clay. Try also opening up the body by adding grog: more open clays are less likely to bloat, so add molochite or fire-brick grog.

■ If the bloating is happening under reduction-firing conditions, it could be because the high iron content in the clay acts as a flux and causes the clay to soften or become pyroplastic sooner than it would under oxidation. Iron is refractory under oxidation but fusible under reduction, resulting in the clay over-firing despite the temperature being the same as in oxidation. Experiment to find the optimum firing temperature or change the clay to a variety with a lower iron content.

■ Loading clay with an oxide such as copper can have the effect of fluxing the clay, thus reducing the temperature at which it matures. If it is then fired at the temperature recommended for the clay, it will appear over-fired and bloating is likely to result. Reduce the top temperature to overcome or slow down the firing a little.

Check the firing cycle

■ If it is overly long, it can cause too much heat work, leading to bloating. A stoneware firing should normally last between 10½ and 13 hours in most studio situations. Conversely, firing too quickly will have the same effect.

■ Most volatiles in a clay body will burn away between 650 and 1000°C (1202 and 1832°F)

if fired properly. Firing at 100°C (212°F) per hour for both biscuit and glost should result in all volatile gases having the chance to escape and make bloating less likely.

Dry your wares: Make sure that all work is absolutely dry before firing. Trapped moisture can cause bloating or explosions as it seeks to escape.

Packing your kiln: Wares tightly packed in electric kilns are more prone to bloating than in gas kilns, so try packing more loosely to allow greater movement of air around the items and avoid placing things too close to the elements to avoid over-firing to one side of the wares.

Copper bloat

Crazing: Problem or decorative effect?

THE PROBLEM

Crazing

Fine cracks in the glaze, usually most pronounced where the glaze is thickest.

Caused by: Difference in contraction between the clay body and glaze covering; moisture expansion in more porous bodies such as terracottas, which swell over time (this is why glaze may craze some time after firing); applying a glaze too thickly; under-firing; firing too quickly; clay – low expansion body; glaze – high expansion; thermal shock (used for effect in raku); the addition of metal oxides to the glaze.

THE SOLUTIONS

Glaze selection: Check that your glaze is the correct type for the body – many glazes are white when they are applied and it is easy to mix up an earthenware glaze with a stoneware!

Firing ranges

- If your clay comes with a recommended firing range, fire it to at least the minimum on the scale to avoid crazing when glazed. Refiring crazed wares within the recommended range for the body will often solve the problem, providing the glaze can also be fired to a higher temperature.
- Aim to glaze fire at 100–120°C (212–248°F) per hour to avoid firing too quickly; refiring wares at this given temperature rate will often resolve a crazing problem.
- Glaze can, for the most part, withstand compression but not expansion. Porous clay bodies absorb moisture over time, which causes it to expand, putting the glaze under tension and thus causing it to craze. Resolve this by increasing the maximum firing temperature.

Alter your body or glaze recipe

Add 5–50 per cent talc to a clay body to reduce moisture expansion (experiment to find the optimum amount) or replace the feldspar content of the body with dolomite and/or talc. (You may need to add a secondary flux also if the clay requires it.)
- Stoneware, porcelain and raku bodies that are glaze fired at earthenware temperatures will usually craze. If higher firing is not an option, try adding flint or cristobalite to the clay body.
- Reduce thermal expansion of the glaze by using low expansion frits (ask your supplier for advice). Or add silica (flint, quartz) plus a small amount of flux (lead bisilicate or borax frit for earthenware, Cornish stone, whiting or dolomite for stoneware) to balance the refractory effect that the addition of silica can have.
- Add up to 5 per cent zircon to the glaze to improve hardness (this amount should not affect opacification, but will reduce thermal expansion).
- Use boric, lead or zinc oxides, zirconia or magnesia instead of alumina, potash or soda.

Be aware that alkaline glazes always craze unless applied very thinly, but using a lithium-based frit will help.
- Always balance added glaze ingredients; if one thing is added, other things have to be adjusted. Adding metallic oxides such as manganese dioxide, iron or copper to glaze can increase thermal expansion: compensate by firing higher or soaking for longer, or, to make the glaze more craze-resistant, add flint, quartz or low-expansion frit.

Glaze application: Apply the glaze more thinly. Oxides can flux glaze considerably, so thick applications fired higher would be inclined to run more than usual.

Avoid thermal shock: Prevent crazing from thermal shock by waiting until the temperature of the kiln has cooled to that of the room before opening. Opening above 100°C (212°F) will almost always result in crazing. The effects of thermal shock are what give raku fired wares their characteristic surfaces.

The crazing in the base of the dish directly relates to the thickness of the glaze.

The crazing in this example is more complex as it spirals around the form, following the throwing direction.

Gaps in the glaze

THE PROBLEM

Crawling

Exposed areas of clay occur where the glaze appears to have withdrawn. The extent of the crawling may vary from large exposed areas to small isolated areas or beading all over the surface. Viscous glazes are more prone to crawling than fluid ones: zircon opacified, matt glazes containing zinc oxide, high alumina and leadless glazes can all be problematic, along with those containing colemenite.

Caused by: A repellent such as oil, wax or dust on the biscuit surface, which prevents the glaze from sticking; knocking the glazed surface prior to firing, which can affect adhesion; firing too quickly and too soon after glazing while the wares are still wet, creating steam that forces the glaze to separate as it escapes (especially in once-fired wares); overly thick glaze application; excessive glaze shrinkage as a result of adding binders such as CMC; underglaze decoration forms a surface too dry for the glaze to adhere or too oily if medium has been used; soluble salts in the clay (especially red types) or in water, causing scumming.

The clay is exposed where the glaze has crawled back.

THE SOLUTIONS

Minimize contact: Avoid handling biscuit wares excessively prior to glazing to prevent transferring oils from the hand to the surface.

Don't wait around: Glaze as soon after biscuit firing as possible, to avoid items gathering dust on a shelf.

Use caution with resists: When using wax or another resist, be careful not to splash it onto surrounding items.

Handle glazed wares with care: Avoid knocking the surface, especially if glaze binders have been used.

Firing alterations

■ Fire once-fired wares very slowly over the first 60°C (111°F) and other wares similarly over the first 100°C (212°F). Make sure wares are thoroughly dry before firing.

■ Try firing underglaze decoration on before glaze firing; this will burn the medium away, thus removing the oiliness. Decorating the clay as an alternative to biscuit can also help.

■ Try biscuit firing a little higher, so that the wares are less porous and take up less glaze.

Adjust your glaze

■ Alter overly viscous glaze by adding extra flux such as borax frit or lead bisilicate, or fire higher.

■ Part replace colemenite with calcium borate frit, or slow down the firing.

■ Add some flux (lead bisilicate or borax frit) to the decorative colour. Commercially bought underglaze colours have flux added, so bond readily and accept glaze better.

■ Add 1–3 per cent glaze binder to the colour pigment (SCMC type).

■ Avoid scumming on the surface of red clays (which can cause glaze to crawl) by adding barium carbonate to the clay body. Also add a drop of vinegar to water when throwing or wiping over surfaces after making.

■ If the glaze is too thick, water it down to the correct consistency. Measuring the pint weight (see page 65) will allow you to correct the glaze mix to its original formula.

■ Don't allow items to linger in the glaze bucket – they should be dipped quickly in and out again.

Importance of kiln placement

THE PROBLEM

Starved glaze

Glossy glaze lacks shine – often in one area only.

Caused by: The item being adjacent to a porous surface in the kiln – new shelf props are often to blame, because they absorb glaze vapour, but unglazed wares fired alongside glazed wares can have the same effect; under-firing; glaze being too thin: Over-firing, causing vaporization of glaze ingredients.

THE SOLUTIONS

Seal props: Coat new props with a wash of china clay and feldspar to seal them (do not use this on shelves, since wares will stick to it).

Separate firings: Avoid firing glazed and non-glazed items together.

Change kiln position: Refire under-fired wares to a higher temperature, in a different position in the kiln to previously.

Double dip: Where possible and the style of glazing allows, re-dip the item in some flocculated glaze. Add a few teaspoons of calcium chloride or magnesium sulphate in solution to a gallon mix of glaze; this should allow even vitrified wares to be re-glazed.

Prevention: Where items have been over-fired, little can be done to solve the problem, but for future firings reduce the length of firing or soak for a shorter period of time.

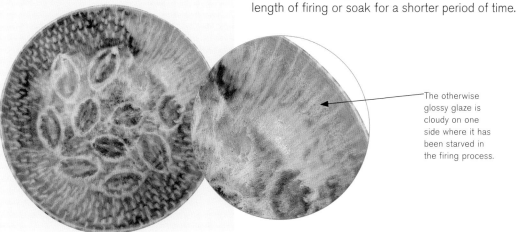

The otherwise glossy glaze is cloudy on one side where it has been starved in the firing process.

Accidental reduction

THE PROBLEM

Milky glaze

Low-temperature transparent lead glaze comes out of the kiln looking opaque and milky.

Caused by: Closing the vents in the kiln too early when using certain black ball clays which contain large amounts of carbonaceous matter – the result being the creation of a reduction atmosphere because the matter has not been able to vent the kiln when burning out; overpacking the kiln.

THE SOLUTION

Know your clay: Be aware of the materials making up your clay body so that special firing requirements can be accommodated.

Keep the kiln vents open: This should be done until at least 600°C (1112°F) to give escaping gases time to vent the kiln; if possible (and not a fire risk), leave open for longer.

Do not overpack the kiln: Give items adequate space for air to move easily around them.

Keep to ramp rates: Fire the wares at the recommended ramp rate for the clay and glaze type. Don't be tempted to speed it up because gases trapped in the clay body could also lead to bloating.

Decorating faults

This section looks at some of the things that can go wrong in the process of applying post-glaze surface treatments and in the clay itself where the decorative detail is created by the inclusion of colour in the form of oxides and stains.

Trouble with agate

THE PROBLEM

Agate warps and bloats

Forms warp and collapse in firing and bloat blisters can be seen in the clay.

Caused by: Oxides acting as a flux in the clay, thereby reducing the maturing temperature so that, when fired to the usual temperature, it is over-fired; manganese is the main culprit in the example below.

Recipes for Coloured Clay

These recipes give some indication of the colours achievable with a limited number of pigments. The amounts shown are for 1 kg (2.2 lb) of white clay. The colours and oxides can be used as they are, or in the combinations listed. Most stains need 10–30 g (0.35–1 oz), depending on the colour strength required. An enormous colour palette can be achieved with a little experimentation.
Body stains: Canary yellow, orange, pink, sky or bright blue, black
Oxides: Cobalt, copper, red iron, manganese

THE SOLUTIONS

Reduce oxide in the clay

Test by making small samples, reducing the amount of oxide in each by very small quantities; number each one and make a corresponding note of the amount. Fire all samples together as recommended next.
■ See chart below for recommended oxide and stain inclusions in clay.
Reduce the top firing temperature: 15–20°C (59–68°F) can make all the difference, but some experimenting may be required. Aim to under-fire first, moving the temperature up by 5°C (41°F) degrees at a time until the optimum is reached.
Support your forms: By placing on either sand or alumina (only if not glazed) to maintain shape and prevent warping or slumping. See Kilns: packing and firing on page 133.

COLOUR	STAIN OR OXIDE	QUANTITY
Blue	Cobalt oxide A little red iron can dull the colour, or copper can add a green tinge	1–10 g (0.03–0.35 oz) (max)
Turquoise	Sky blue Canary yellow	10 g (0.35 oz) 20 g (0.7 oz)
Bright green	Sky blue Canary yellow	20 g (0.7 oz) 30 g (1 oz)
Light olive green	Egg yellow stain Cobalt oxide	10 g (0.35 oz) 2 g (0.07 oz)
Dark olive green	Egg yellow stain Cobalt oxide	10 g (0.35 oz) 4 g (0.14 oz)
Mustard	Orange stain Red iron oxide	20 g (0.7 oz) 8 g (0.3 oz)
Light purple	Pink stain Cobalt oxide	25 g (0.9 oz) 2 g (0.07 oz)
Dark purple	Pink stain Cobalt oxide	25 g (0.9 oz) 4 g (0.14 oz)
Khaki or green	Copper oxide gives khaki without glaze; green with glaze	10–25 g (0.35 oz–0.9 oz)
Black (A)	Black body stain	45 g (1.5 oz)
Black (B)	Cobalt oxide Copper carbonate Manganese dioxide	15 g (0.5 oz) 15 g (0.5 oz) 15 g (0.5 oz)

Protecting the agate surface

THE PROBLEM

Poor surface finish

Inability to achieve a smooth surface when fettling prior to firing; refining at the dry stage results in the ware breaking because it is made up from so many component parts and is too delicate to handle. This problem is particularly relevant in moulded items.

Caused by: The nature of the construction making the item delicate to handle at the clay stage; insufficient slip used to join the agate sections together; bad technique when scraping away excess slip after removing the item from the mould; scraping the surface either before it is sufficiently dry or when too dry.

THE SOLUTIONS

Optimum dryness: Wait until the form is just a little drier than leather hard but not completely dry before scraping the surface to remove excess slip.

Best tool: Use a metal kidney to scrape the surface. Try not to gouge it into the clay, but draw it gently over the surface with as much of the metal in contact as possible. Support the surface being scraped on the underside.

Refire: If the surface is still uneven after scraping, low biscuit fire the form to 900°C (1652°F). This will allow the surface to be sanded easily without the form breaking. Using wet-and-dry sandpaper in successively fine grades, dampen the surface and sand back. This is also a good way of thinning the walls if they are a little too thick. Allow to dry out thoroughly before firing to top temperature. **(1)**

Note: Even though working with wet-and-dry sandpaper minimizes dust, wear a dust mask for safety.

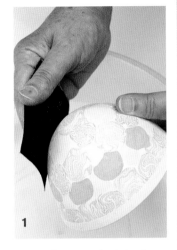

1

Hold the form over a bowl of water when sanding and wash the surface when finished. Allow to dry thoroughly before refiring.

Bad lustre colour

THE PROBLEM

Gold lustre looks purple

Gold lustre decoration looks patchy and mostly purple after firing on.

Caused by: The lustre being applied too thinly; too much thinning agent; temperature too high; contamination from brushes and other sources.

THE SOLUTIONS

Brush on an even coat: It should look tan in colour when dry. If it is applied too thickly, it will blister in firing; if applied too thinly, the purple colour will result.

Stir thoroughly before using: A glass or plastic rod is the best tool for mixing liquid gold as it avoids wastage. Use the brush to clean the excess off the rods afterwards.

Keep brushes separate and clean: Brushes used to apply gold should never be used to apply other colours. Painting a mark on the brush with a gold marker pen will ensure that you can identify it next time. Use gold thinners or lavender oil to clean your brushes.

Firing gold: The optimum temperature to fire gold lies somewhere between 700 and 750°C (1292 and 1382°F). Much depends on the kiln – some experimentation may be required to find the correct temperature for yours. Start at the lower end of the range and work up until you achieve the correct firing.

The lustre has fired patchily and looks purple in places rather than gold.

Inconsistent lustre colour

THE PROBLEM

Patchy lustre

The lustre coat is inconsistent. Colours are indistinct, not firing true.

Caused by: Method of application, especially where sponges are used; the application being too thin; over-firing, resulting in colours burning out; inadequate ventilation causing

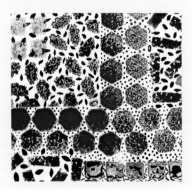

THE SOLUTIONS

■ See Gold lustre looks purple, page 109; many of the solutions also apply here.
Be prepared: Have all your colours, brushes and thinners in place before you begin.
Sponging lustre
1 Pour just a little onto a spare tile, then dip the sponge in it. The first impression on the surface will be heavier than subsequent impressions. Re-dip the sponge regularly to maintain an even coat. Do not use the sponge for other colours.
2 If the sponged lustre looks too patchy, work over the lustre with a brush to even it out.
Leave to dry: Allow lustre to dry naturally before firing.
Good ventilation of the kiln: This is vital when firing lustres. Hazy or dull, matt colours can result if ventilation is inadequate. Vents can be left open for the entirety of low firings, but if the kiln is in the studio, it must also be thoroughly ventilated so that you do not breathe in fumes. It is better not to be in there at the same time.

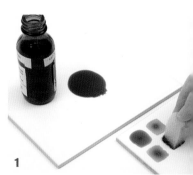

1

2

Applying decals

THE PROBLEM

Holes in decals

The fired decal has holes in where it has not adhered to the surface. It feels rough and can look as though it has crawled back.

Caused by: Poor application technique, resulting in water being trapped. During firing the water converts to steam, causing the decal to blow out as it escapes.

THE SOLUTIONS

Decal application
1 Ease the decal onto the surface in a rolling kind of action from bottom to top. This way, the water will be forced upward and away as the design is positioned.
2 Once the decal is in place, run a flexible rubber kidney over it to force out any water that may be trapped underneath.
3 Finish off by wiping over the decal with a sponge to mop up remaining water
4 Allow the decal to dry thoroughly before firing.
Cover the damage: If the decal blowout is not too serious and the design allows it, consider adding some lustre detail in the damaged areas to hide it and fire again.

1

2

Last resort solutions

We have all opened a kiln with anticipation of great things, only to be bitterly disappointed – but providing the work is still intact, there are things that can still be done to change the appearance and transform the surface.

Grinding: sand blasting

This may be an extreme length to go to, but many surface defects can be erased by grinding them away. Often, unexpected and exciting qualities can be created or exposed in the process.

Use to: Remove surface defects (even glaze can be ground away); create a contrasting surface quality; polish a surface.
Equipment: Use a commercial grinder (these can be hired for a day if required). Choose a type that sends a constant flow of water over the grinding head if possible so that no dust is produced. If this type is not available, you must wear protective breathing apparatus and goggles.

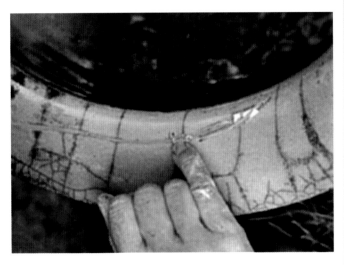

Fill any little cracks or defects with metal leaf to add an exciting new dimension to the form.

Flat surfaces are relatively easy to grind down but other forms may need to be held in a vice to prevent them moving about when working on them.

Apply metal leaf

Used here as a positive design feature and very much part of the potter's signature, this is also a great way to transform a surface that needs a little something else to lift it.

Use to: Fill cracks; cover over surface blemishes; add a precious touch to an otherwise ordinary form.
Technique: Paint a thin coat of gold size over the chosen area, then wait until it becomes sticky. Press the metal leaf onto the size, then burnish to buff up the sheen. A soft brush can be used to remove excess leaf; store the brushed-off bits to use again at a later date.

Try also:

- When the form is good but the glaze is dull, try painting on enamel or lustre decoration to make the glaze look as if it was a deliberate choice as a background.
- Decals can also lift a surface. Use to cover the whole surface or just in selected areas to cover up specific defects or in combination with enamels or lustres.
- Apply another glaze in a contrasting colour. The glaze will need a CMC binder adding to make it stick to an already glazed surface, but interesting effects can be achieved with creative applications.
- Create stripes using masking paper as a resist.
- Stencil the secondary glaze on in patterns.

CHAPTER 5

FIRING

IT WON'T MATTER HOW WELL ITEMS HAVE BEEN MADE AND
DECORATED IF THEY ARE FIRED INCORRECTLY. THEREFORE
A GOOD UNDERSTANDING OF CORRECT PROCEDURES
WILL GO A LONG WAY TO AVOIDING PROBLEMS. ALL THE
INFORMATION REQUIRED FOR GOOD FIRING PRACTICE IS
CONTAINED IN THIS CHAPTER, INCLUDING FIX-ITS FOR LOW
FIRING TECHNIQUES.

Firing

The fundamental item of equipment for the potter is, of course, the kiln, and choosing the right one will be determined by several factors, including the size and type of work you wish to make, the space available to house the kiln and the type of fuel you wish to use. The choice is huge, and you would be well advised to speak to other potters and manufacturers to find the type that will best meet your needs.

What type of kiln?

This section gives the pros and cons for each type of kiln, highlighting the special requirements and considerations for different firing methods.

ELECTRIC KILNS

Pros

- Electricity is available to almost everyone and provides a clean, efficient, stable and reliable way of firing.
- Kilns are available in a good range of sizes; the smaller ones can be plugged into a domestic socket and are therefore easily sited.
- Electric kilns have good temperature control, especially with modern digital controllers that regulate every part of the firing and switch the kiln off when it reaches the temperature that has been preset.

- Electricity burns cleanly, so emissions are less harmful to the environment.

Cons

- This type of firing lacks the sensory, hands-on experience of many other firing methods, especially those where the kiln requires feeding with fuel to maintain temperature.
- Some special surface effects are unachievable in electric kilns, although there are now a good many products available that can help achieve similar effects and books available on exciting electric firing.

▶ Front-loading kilns have a very solid metal frame and thicker walls than the top-loading variety, which means they retain heat for longer. They are very hard-wearing, but more expensive to buy and install and also very heavy, so thought must go into siting them.

◀ Top-loading kilns are perfect for smaller workshops because they are cheap to buy and easy to install (some even plug in to a domestic socket). Top loaders tend to cool much faster than front loaders which can sometimes have a detrimental effect on the work but for many potters this is an advantage because the kiln allows for a very quick firing cycle.

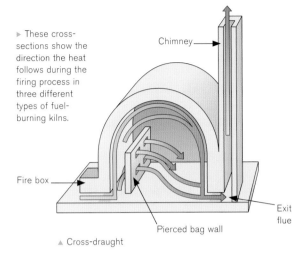

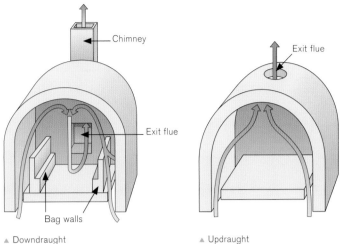

▶ These cross-sections show the direction the heat follows during the firing process in three different types of fuel-burning kilns.

Chimney

Fire box

Pierced bag wall

Exit flue

▲ Cross-draught

Chimney

Exit flue

Bag walls

▲ Downdraught

Exit flue

▲ Updraught

FUEL-BURNING KILNS

There are three design types – updraught, downdraught, and cross-draught.

Updraught kilns The fire is below the chamber or at the lower end. The heat rises up through the chamber to exit via a chimney or flue at the top. There are some problems attached to this type of kiln because there are always hot spots, depending on how the heat travels through the chamber to the exit hole. Considerate packing is vital.

Downdraught kilns The fire enters the chamber from the base or sides of the kiln. It is drawn up or deflected by an internal structure called a bag wall, which forces the heat up to the ceiling and back down again into the chamber, finally exiting via a flue at the back into another chamber or a chimney. This type of kiln allows higher temperature firings in oxidation or reduction and is a more efficient kiln type than an updraught.

Cross-draught kilns The fuel is introduced at one side of the entrance via a stoke hole or fire box, causing the heat to circulate in a crisscross fashion to the top of the kiln then back down through the chamber, exiting through a flue on the opposite side to the stoke hole. This kiln design has been used to developed tube or bank kilns and climbing chamber kilns.

GAS KILNS (INCLUDING RAKU KILNS)

Pros

- Can be fired safely in a building with plenty of space around it or under cover outside.
- This is the firing method that should be used for reduction wares.
- Small kilns can be made from simple materials like ceramic fibre; larger ones will require fire bricks and fibre but can be site specific.
- A fire brick kiln should last five years and allow approximately 250 firings before it has to be rebuilt.
- Gas supply can be mains, propane bottle or tank.
- Raku is an exciting, interactive firing technique producing exciting results very quickly.

Cons

- The siting of gas kilns, except for raku kilns, is controlled by local planning restrictions and regulations.
- Raku firing requires extra equipment for post-firing treatments. It can be hazardous to health through breathing in fumes because it is an interactive firing technique.
- Insurance may be higher because of fire risk and emissions.
- Consideration must be given to neighbours when siting gas kilns because of the nuisance of smoke and emissions.
- There is no advantage to biscuit firing in a gas kiln so electric kilns are often used as well – an extra expense.
- Pipe work needs to be professionally installed and the gas supply sited away from the kiln.

WOOD-BURNING KILNS

Pros

- Glazes have a visual softness, created by the combined effects of wood smoke, ash and the gases given off during firing.
- A wide variety of surface effects can be achieved depending on wood type and firing cycle.

Cons

- A lengthy firing cycle requires constant attention to feed the kiln.
- A large supply of wood is required; it must be seasoned and dry to burn well.
- The kiln has to be built; it is site specific and requires someone experienced to construct it.
- A mixture of soft and hard wood is required.
- It produces a lot of smoke, and is therefore not suitable for urban areas.

OIL-FIRED KILNS

See gas kilns.
In addition, oil-fired kilns are usually gravity fed, so the fuel supply must be higher than the burners and sited well away from the kiln.

SAWDUST KILNS

Pros

- An inexpensive method of firing to achieve exciting surface effects.
- Only requires a metal bin to get started but kilns can be temporarily built from house bricks and relocated if required.
- Once ignited, the kiln can be left to burn down without further attention.
- Other combustibles can be used as an alternative fuel – for example, newspaper, straw, peat, dung.

Cons

- The temperature will never get high enough to biscuit fire, so an electric kiln is required as well.
- Smoke nuisance to neighbours.

PAPER KILNS

Pros

- Can be a theatrical way of firing – good for experimentation.
- Paper is an inexpensive and readily available material.
- Temperatures of up to 1150°C (2102°F) can be achieved if constructed well.
- Structures can be built from rolled and twisted paper and wire or from timber and paper covered with china clay.

Cons

- Paper kilns only fire once; they must be rebuilt each firing.

◄ This kiln is made by tightly rolling and folding layers of paper, bound together with more rolled paper to form a container. The cavity is packed with one or more pots, as well as other combustible materials to create interesting marks, then set alight from the base – they can take a surprisingly long time to burn away completely.

TYPICAL BISCUIT-FIRING SCHEDULE

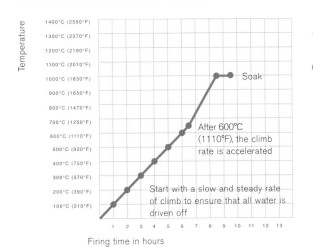

Soak

After 600°C (1110°F), the climb rate is accelerated

Start with a slow and steady rate of climb to ensure that all water is driven off

Firing time in hours

TYPICAL STONEWARE SCHEDULE

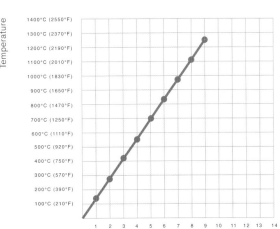

Firing time in hours

Measuring temperature – the options

There are several ways of measuring and controlling the temperature of the kiln as it fires; the following section shows the options available.

DIGITAL PROGRAMME CONTROLLERS

Most modern electric and gas kilns come with a digital programmer, which is very simple and convenient to use because it allows the firing schedule to be set at stages or ramps, which change automatically and then switch off. More sophisticated controllers allow for staged ramps, both rising and falling, so that cooling can be controlled as well as heating. In addition, some have features that control an electronic damper, which can be set to close at a set temperature.

Choose a digital programmer if you want to feel confident about leaving the kiln to fire itself. An added safety feature can include a safety over-fire device, which would shut down the kiln if it fired beyond the preset number of hours.

PYROMETRIC CONES

Triangular in shape, pyrometric cones are made from materials that will bend at given temperatures. They are numbered to show their specific bending temperature; different brands have different numbers.

Cones should be placed in a row of three within sight through the spy holes of the kiln; larger kilns may require cones at both the top and bottom of the kiln to determine an even firing.

Using cones requires being on hand periodically to check the temperature for putting bungs in, shutting the firing down, etc. Used more in flame firings, they are also useful for checking that a kiln is firing evenly if problems arise.

◀ Pyrometric cones bend as the heat rises in the kiln. Cones are a very reliable way of gauging kiln temperature. The melted cones demonstrate how the correct temperature is measured when the last one just begins to bend at 1300°C (2370°F).

1300°C (2370°F)   1290°C (2350°F)   1280°C (2340°F)

THERMOCOUPLES AND PYROMETERS

Pyrometers are devices that show the rise and fall of temperature on a display and are connected to a thermocouple (a long, thin ceramic probe that protrudes into the kiln), which takes the temperature.

Pyrometers are generally fixed in position, but are also available as mobile devices. These are useful for measuring temperature in certain types of firing such as raku or saggar firing in raku kilns, where careful temperature control is critical to the finish.

Older electric kilns may have simple dial controllers that may read off/low/medium/high or 0–100. They can be used in combination with both pyrometric cones and pyrometers and thermocouples, but you will need to be on hand to change the temperature and switch off unless a cutoff switch is attached to the pyrometer.

DRAW RINGS

Used mainly in wood, salt and soda glazing, draw rings are made from the same clay and glaze as the work in the kiln and are drawn out periodically with an iron rod to check the progress of the firing. They are a very efficient way of measuring heat in these types of firing.

Things to be aware of when firing

Kilns vary widely in the way they fire and many things can affect the firing, including the kiln furniture! Being aware of these issues will enable a more considered approach to packing the kiln and hopefully will allow you to avoid the associated problems.

TEMPERATURE GRADIENTS

When firing, the temperature of a kiln bat lags behind the rising temperature in the kiln air. The bases of wares sitting on the bat are therefore chilled through conduction, creating a temperature gradient through the form from base to top.

Conversely, when the kiln is shut off and the temperature begins to cool, the opposite happens: the bat retains heat, keeping the base hotter than the rapidly cooling top.

Given that the clay at the top of the form will go through the silica inversions before the clay at the base, the wares are placed under stress. One way to overcome the issue is to prop the work so that it doesn't come into contact with the bat – but this is not possible for stoneware firings because the supports would cause the clay to distort as it became pyroplastic. Flat slabs or strips of biscuit clay can be used where props are not practical (firing platforms).

HEAT TRANSMISSION

In electric firings, heat is transmitted mainly by radiation, so pots in the centre of a dense load are shadowed by those surrounding them, causing another temperature lag. Often wares can under-fire in this situation, compared to those nearer the elements, so remembering how the kiln has been packed can help you quickly identify the cause of such a problem.

ELEMENTS

Wares standing next to elements will incline towards the heat source, shrinking more on the surface closest than on the side in shadow.

Downdraught gas and oil kilns suffer less from this problem because the heat is transmitted more directly to the wares through conduction and convection.

SIZE AND SHAPE

Further stresses and inequality of firing are determined by the size, shape and thickness of pieces being fired and consideration of placing should be given to a load to get the best results. Generally, the faster the firing cycle, the less evenly wares will fire.

Soaking at the top temperature is a useful way of evening out the various stress factors in a firing, especially where there is a discrepancy in size and thickness of wares.

Alternative firing methods: Low firing

Really, low firing is an experimental journey for most potters for which there is no real best practice. Many of the problems encountered can only be resolved through trial and error because they are unique to the individual firing circumstances, but there are a few useful tips that you can use as a starting point, andwhich will help you to understand where things can go wrong.

TOOLS AND EQUIPMENT

Many potters start out low firing because, once the kiln has been purchased, it requires a minimum outlay but it still gives scope for great experimentation in surface treatment.

Kilns or firing chambers can be made from house bricks, metal bins, old oil containers, ceramic fibre and wire; even old electric kilns can be put to use once disconnected, providing they can be re-sited easily.

Few tools are required beyond those used in other firing techniques, but good, thick kiln gloves will allow you to handle wares that need turning in the firing chamber if demanded and raku-type tongs are good for lifting items out of combustibles to avoid fire risk.

A respirator should be used to avoid breathing in fumes (more important for some techniques than others). Goggles and other protective facial wear are also advised for health and safety purposes.

COMBUSTIBLES

Experiment with sawdust, wood shavings, straw, newspaper and hair, or organic materials such as leaves, banana skins, nut shells and seaweed. You can also alternate sawdust with other combustibles for more interesting surface effects.

Pack wares in sawdust until covered, then set alight from the top, using paper to get the fire started. When burning well, clamp down a lid that allows just a little through draught and allow to smoke until the sawdust burns away.

If you are using only newspaper it will take several refirings to get the required result. You will need a large supply of newspaper; tabloids burn better than broad sheets.

MASKING MATERIALS

There are several materials that can be used to mask wares prior to firing: Paper tapes (cut into fine lines for detail work or shapes for larger patterns); wax; latex and other commercial masking fluids, including certain glues; clay, clay slurries and slips, china clay/flint slip for applying underglaze for resist raku, etc. Some of these masking materials are more suitable than others for certain techniques, but trial and error is useful in this instance and fantastic results can be achieved by combining masking materials.

Useful tips for low firing

- For many low-fire techniques, a burnished surface will give a much better outcome than just plain clay, both visually and from a tactile point of view.
- Do not biscuit fire burnished wares above 1000°C (1832°F), otherwise the sheen will be lost.
- Slurries to be used over masking paper pattern are best made from grogged clay to prevent them firing on; grog can be added to a general slip or clay body to make the slurry as an alternative.
- Very thin wares are difficult to smoke using slurry resist because they do not have the thickness for absorbtion and the slurry will therefore peel off.
- Higher fired wares will reject slurry also because of lack of porosity in the body, and sometimes highly burnished items can be problematical for the same reason, along with surfaces covered with terrasigillata.
- Avoid soft woods where possible if using sawdust because they are particularly resinous and can mark the clay; biscuit firing again will usually resolve the problem if it occurs.
- Over-firing can cause slurry to fuse with the clay body. Sometimes soaking in water prior to removing the slip will help, but experience will usually teach you to recognize the best time to cease firing using this technique.

Orton pyrometric cone temperatures

These tables provide a guide for selecting cones. The actual bending temperature depends on firing conditions. Temperatures shown are for specific mounted height above base. For self-supporting – 4.5 cm (1¾ in); for large – 5.1 cm (2 in); for small – 2.4 cm ($^{15}/_{16}$ in). For large cones mounted at 4.5 cm (1¾ in) height, use self-supporting temperatures.

	Self-Supporting Cones						Large Cones			
	Regular			Iron Free			Regular		Iron Free	
	Heating Rate °C/hour									
	15	60	150	15	60	150	60	150	60	150
Firing speed	Slow	Medium	Fast	Slow	Medium	Fast	Medium	Fast	Medium	Fast
Cone #										
022		586	590							
021		600	617							
20		626	638							
019	656	678	695				676	693		
018	686	715	734				712	732		
017	705	738	763				736	761		
016	742	772	796				769	794		
015	750	791	818				788	816		
014	757	807	838				807	836		
013	807	837	861				837	859		
012	843	861	882				858	880		
011	857	875	894				873	892		
010	891	903	915	871	886	893	898	913	884	891
09	907	920	930	899	919	928	917	928	917	926
08	922	942	956	924	946	957	942	954	945	955
07	962	976	987	953	971	982	973	985	970	980
06	981	998	1013	969	991	998	995	1011	991	996
05.5	1004	1015	1025	990	1012	1021	1012	1023	1011	1020
05	1021	1031	1044	1013	1037	1046	1030	1046	1032	1044
04	1046	1063	1077	1043	1061	1069	1060	1070	1060	1067
03	1071	1086	1104	1066	1088	1093	1086	1101	1087	1091
02	1078	1102	1122	1084	1105	1115	1101	1120	1102	1113
01	1093	1119	1138	1101	1123	1134	1117	1137	1122	1132
1	1109	1137	1154	1119	1139	1148	1136	1154	1137	1146
2	1112	1142	1164				1142	1162		
3	1115	1152	1170	1130	1154	1162	1152	1168	1151	1160
4	1141	1162	1183				1160	1181		
5	1159	1186	1207				1184	1205		
5.5	1167	1203	1225							
6	1185	1222	1243				1220	1241		
7	1201	1239	1257				1237	1255		
8	1211	1249	1271				1247	1269		
9	1224	1260	1280				1257	1278		
10	1251	1285	1305				1282	1303		
11	1272	1294	1315				1293	1312		
12	1285	1306	1326				1304	1324		
13*	1309	1331	1348				1321	1346		
14*	1351	1365	1384				1388	1366		

Colour designation key

- [ ] Denotes the regular cone series
- [shaded] Cones made with red iron oxide
- [ ] Cones made without iron oxide

*The large differences in temperature equivalents between self-supporting and large cones 13 and 14 is due to different compositions.

	Self-Supporting Cones						Large Cones			
	Regular			Iron Free			Regular		Iron Free	
	Heating Rate °F/hour									
	27	108	270	27	108	270	108	270	108	270
Firing speed	Slow	Medium	Fast	Slow	Medium	Fast	Medium	Fast	Medium	Fast
Cone #										
022		1087	1094							
021		1112	1143							
20		1159	1180							
019	1213	1252	1283				1249	1279		
018	1267	1319	1353				1314	1350		
017	1301	1360	1405				1357	1402		
016	1368	1422	1465				1416	1461		
015	1382	1456	1504				1450	1501		
014	1395	1485	1540				1485	1537		
013	1485	1539	1582				1539	1578		
012	1549	1582	1620				1576	1616		
011	1575	1607	1641				1603	1638		
010	1636	1657	1679	1600	1627	1639	1648	1675	1623	1636
09	1665	1688	1706	1650	1686	1702	1683	1702	1683	1699
08	1692	1728	1753	1695	1735	1755	1728	1749	1733	1751
07	1764	1789	1809	1747	1780	1800	1783	1805	1778	1796
06	1798	1828	1855	1776	1816	1828	1823	1852	1816	1825
05.5	1839	1859	1877	1814	1854	1870	1854	1873	1852	1868
05	1870	1888	1911	1855	1899	1915	1886	1915	1890	1911
04	1915	1945	1971	1909	1942	1956	1940	1958	1940	1953
03	1960	1987	2019	1951	1990	1999	1987	2014	1989	1996
02	1972	2016	2052	1983	2021	2039	2014	2048	2016	2035
01	1999	2046	2080	2014	2053	2073	2043	2079	2052	2070
1	2028	2079	2109	2046	2082	2098	2077	2109	2079	2095
2	2034	2088	2127				2088	2124		
3	2039	2106	2138	2066	2109	2124	2106	2134	2104	2120
4	2086	2124	2161				2120	2158		
5	2118	2167	2205				2163	2201		
5.5	2133	2197	2237							
6	2165	2232	2269				2228	2266		
7	2194	2262	2295				2259	2291		
8	2212	2280	2320				2277	2316		
9	2235	2300	2336				2295	2332		
10	2284	2345	2381				2340	2377		
11	2322	2361	2399				2359	2394		
12	2345	2383	2419				2379	2415		
13*	2389	2428	2458				2410*	2455*		
14*	2464	2489	2523				2530*	2491*		

Kiln housekeeping

You will no doubt be familiar with the various items of kiln furniture available for creating levels and supporting work in firing, so for best practice here it would seem most useful to suggest ways of placing or setting work to minimize problems. However, there are a few basic essentials it is useful to be aware of when packing.

▲ Wares packed in ready for biscuit firing.

Packing for a biscuit firing

It is important to make maximum use of the internal space of your kiln for cost purposes and fuel efficiency. Work out in advance which wares can be packed inside other items and how they can fit alongside each other, but be conscious not to put undue stress on any form because they are at their most vulnerable at this stage. Tiles can be stacked upright, small objects placed inside others. Plates and flatwares can be stacked. Place the heaviest items at the bottom of the kiln with the lightest at the top. Be conscious of your back in the packing process so that you don't have to reach into the back of the kiln for heavy or difficult shapes. Make the packing easy for yourself when loading and unloading.

Packing for glaze firing

Glazed wares must be packed further apart than biscuit wares because items can easily stick together as the glaze cools after firing. The following points should help avoid this and other problems associated with glaze packing:

- Work must not touch in glaze firing – allow 2 cm (¾ in) around each item to allow for glaze bubbling and expansion.
- Make sure all glazed wares have clean bases, otherwise they will stick to the kiln bat.
- Spread silica sand thinly over kiln shelves for high firings to prevent bases from fusing to the kiln shelf; it acts like tiny ball bearings, allowing the items to move during shrinkage.
- Alumina – the main ingredient in bat wash – prevents clay and glaze from sticking to kiln shelves. It can also be used for placing wares to prevent distortion and is commonly used in bone china firings. Be careful not to spread it too close to the edge of the bat or it will fall onto wares below and seal into a glazed surface.

◄ Packed glazed work prepared for firing.

Packing and unpacking the kiln

The following points apply when packing for both biscuit and glost firing.

- Pieces of greenware can touch each other in biscuit firing.
- Three props, giving triangular support, are best for kiln shelves and they should stack vertically on top of one another.
- Place work at least 4 cm (1½ in) away from elements.
- Allow a good gap between flatwork and the shelf above.
- Heavy work is best placed at the bottom of the kiln.
- Split shelving should be offset at varying levels to allow proper circulation of heat.
- Don't place kiln shelves close together at the base of the kiln, leaving a big gap at the top; this will cause a heat gradient that can lead to over-firing at the base because the thermocouple is usually situated at the top.
- Do not remove bungs until the temperature is below 200°C (390°F).
- Do not crank the kiln door open before 150°C (300°F) and then only by a little to allow the kiln to cool a little faster.
- Wait until the temperature is well below 100°C (212°F) before opening fully to avoid dunting and thermal shock; below 50°C (92°F) is preferable.
- Wear gloves to unpack if the wares are still hot.

Supporting work in the kiln

Certain items, such as figurative wares and sculptures, may need to be supported during firing to prevent them from sagging and warping. This is especially the case with bone china because props must shrink at the same rate as the item being supported to maintain its shape.

- Clay props can be made from the same clay as the body to support figurative work in firing. The point of contact between prop and body should be coated with calcined alumina to prevent the surfaces from sticking together.
- Fire large items and figurative work on shrinkage platforms (sheets of clay larger than the base of the wares); these shrink at the same rate as the item being supported and reduce warping.

▼ Tile crank

▼ Firing stilts

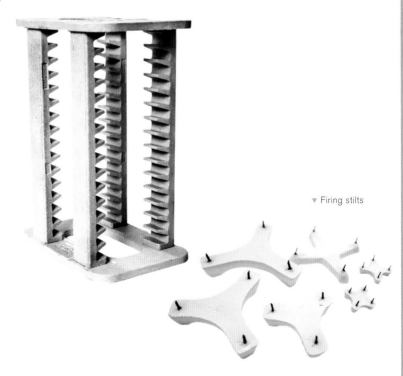

123

Low firing problems

There are no rights and wrongs with smoke firing: it is a journey of discovery. In a way, it is good when things don't work as expected, as these are the things that make us experiment to get a better outcome. However, there are a few problems that can be remedied to help you on your way.

Working with slip resists

THE PROBLEM

Peeling resist slip

Slip used in combination with a masking-tape resist will not adhere to the surface of the biscuit-fired form and peels away as it begins to dry out.

Caused by: Biscuit firing is too high; the burnish is so good that it seals the surface too well (noticeable with terra sigillata) and the resist slip just can't adhere; difference between the shrinkage rate of the clay body and the resist slip; a very thin clay wall being unable to tolerate the covering slip – this applies often with thin porcelain.

THE SOLUTIONS

Lower the temperature: Lower the biscuit firing to 900–960°C (1652–1760°F) for all low-firing techniques, including raku. Simply lowering the firing temperature should help to overcome the lack of porosity and thus allow the resist to stick.

Thorough burnish: A good burnish is always desirable, so aim for the best surface possible.

Clay selection: Use a very grogged clay to make the resist slip – a stoneware grogged clay such as raku body or craft crank is ideal. The slip should actually be more of a slurry than a slip – the thickness of double cream.

Using slurry

■ If the slurry refuses to stick despite all efforts, try adding a small amount of a starchy glue, like wallpaper paste, to the mixture – this should burn away easily in firing and therefore not affect the final surface.

■ Make sure that the slurry is applied evenly and quite thickly to completely obscure the paper resist underneath. Work the brush over the surface in several directions to build up the thickness, otherwise smoke marks that look like brush marks will result.

■ Make the slurry from the same body as the clay, but add grog to open it up a little; this should help to overcome the shrinkage mismatch with porcelains and finer clay bodies.

Remove the cracked, unfired slip and apply a new coat containing a small amount of starchy glue. Work the brush in different directions to build up an even covering – allow the form to dry slowly before firing.

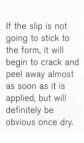

If the slip is not going to stick to the form, it will begin to crack and peel away almost as soon as it is applied, but will definitely be obvious once dry.

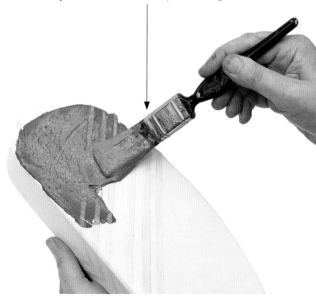

Firing with slip resist

THE PROBLEM

Poor adhesion of slip resist

The slip cracks and falls away in firing, before the form is properly finished.

Caused by: Particular problem with this method of firing, especially where paper is used, because it burns fiercely; the wares are handled more than if fired in sawdust, making them more vulnerable; the masking-tape pattern can lift as it burns away, in turn causing the slurry to break away.

After its initial firing in newspaper, the slip is beginning to lift and is vulnerable to being knocked off. Smoke will seep under the cracks to create darker areas and blur the pattern on the form unless the cracks are sealed before refiring.

THE SOLUTION

Firing in newspaper

1 Using newspaper as the combustible material gives you greater control over the firing outcome and results in a more even design surface finish than if fired in sawdust, although it is more labour-intensive.

2 Firing in newspaper will require packing and firing the kiln several times, and the form must be lifted out each time. Use heatproof gloves to remove the form really carefully to avoid knocking the slip and place it somewhere where you can inspect it.

3 If the slurry looks as though it is lifting, dab on some more to seal the problem; this requires delicacy of touch. The slurry will dry very quickly because the form is hot.

4 If the slurry falls away completely and the pattern underneath has not fired to your satisfaction, simply remove the rest of it, reapply the paper design and slurry, and fire again. Repeat until you are happy with the results.

125

Preparing the kiln for firing

THE PROBLEM

Difficulty getting combustibles to burn

Instead of burning fiercely as required, the kiln just smoulders and makes a lot of smoke, so the paper pattern on the pot does not burn away. The clay surface can also appear adversely smoky, despite the paper not burning away.

Caused by: Poor kiln design – not allowing sufficient air flow to burn well (important where using paper as a combustible); packing the paper too tightly.

THE SOLUTION

Packing your kiln method

1 Drill a series of five or six holes in the base of the metal dustbin and another set of six around the sides of the bin about 5 cm (2 in) from the base.

2 Place three 15-cm (6-in) kiln props inside the bin and rest an open-mesh, metal garden sieve over it.

3 Very loosely pack some scrunched newspaper under the mesh, then fill the bin with more paper.

4 Fire only one pot at a time. Place it in the centre of the bin, loosely pack with paper, and light from the top. Avoid scrunching the newspaper into tight balls; the looser the better to allow free air flow and burn. You will need to refire several times to achieve the best effect.

5 Allow the paper to burn away completely before lifting the form out for inspection and refiring. Use heatproof gloves and handle the form carefully to avoid knocking the slip off.

Safety when firing

THE PROBLEM

Fire

....

Caused by: Burning paper blowing out of the kiln.

THE SOLUTION

Fire prevention: Place a wire mesh over the kiln as it burns – chicken wire or an old metal fireguard work well.

. . . .

Cleaning the fired surface

THE PROBLEM

Stubborn resist slip

....

The slip is difficult to remove after firing without scratching the clay surface and destroying the burnish.

Caused by: Applying the resist slip too thinly; over-firing, causing the slip to fuse to the clay surface; not using a suitably grogged slip; using a slip made from the same clay as the body.

Most of the slip has shelled away cleanly from the surface, leaving just a small area that can't be easily removed.

THE SOLUTIONS

Slip thickness: Aim to achieve a thickness of 2–4 mm ($\frac{1}{16}$–$\frac{1}{8}$ in) when applying the resist slip. The thicker the coating, the easier it will be to remove afterwards. Masking-paper designs underneath the slip should be completely covered.

Monitor slip colour: The resist slip will blacken more with each successive firing. Each time it is removed from the kiln for repacking, check that the slip is not becoming shiny black with a petrol-like sheen on it; this is an indication that it is over-firing. Stop at this point and remove all the slip to see what the firing is like; if necessary, repattern and slip, then refire.

Add grog: If you are using a slip made from the same clay as the body, it must be opened up by adding grog or sand, otherwise it will fuse. Add enough to replicate a very grogged clay like raku body or craft crank.

Soak the form: It is unlikely that firing with paper is going to result in the temperature getting much above 600°C (1112°F), so in theory the clay should not be so fired that it is no longer porous. If careful chipping does not remove the excess slip, try soaking the whole form in warm water for a couple of hours; the remaining slip should then come away easily. Dry the form out thoroughly before polishing with wax.

Low firing problems continued

The dangers of smoke firing

THE PROBLEM

Accidental fire when using a quick smoking method

When spirit-soaked sawdust is placed on the surface of a form, and then set alight to create special smoke effects, the sawdust container is accidentally set on fire.

Caused by: Moist sawdust sticking to the utensil used to transfer it from container to surface. If the same utensil is also used to move the burning sawdust around on the clay surface it gets very hot – so when it is placed back in the container to transfer more sawdust to the surface, it ignites.

THE SOLUTIONS

Prepare your workspace and materials

■ Sit the form to be fired on a kiln bat because it will get very hot; alternatively, support it on a wad of ceramic fibre blanket. **(1)**
■ Use a metal container for the spirit-soaked sawdust – never a plastic container.
■ Use only metal spoons or utensils to transfer the sawdust.

■ Wear gauntlets or heat-protective gloves and avoid the sawdust coming into contact with clothes. **(2)**
■ Avoid using the same utensil to transfer the sawdust and move the sawdust around on the pot surface. Have two or more utensils available and keep their use separate.

■ Avoid having the container of sawdust in close proximity to where you are firing. **(3)**
■ Have a bucket of water on hand.

■ Have a spare bat available next to the container of sawdust. If the sawdust ignites, quickly cover the burning container with the bat. The fire will quickly subside. **(4)**

Alternative saggars

THE PROBLEM

Disappointing tin foil saggar results

Aluminium foil saggars are a quick solution when a clay saggar is not available, but they burn away, leaving a mess and the work shows only black carbon marks, despite packing with varying combustibles.

Caused by: Aluminium foil starts to burn away between 650 and 700°C (1202 and 1292°F), so it is really only suitable for relatively low-smoking effects. This type of saggar is often used in combination with ferric chloride, which is sprayed or painted onto the wares prior to packing in the foil. It gives wonderful pinks, but is very dangerous and not environmentally friendly to use.

Note: Dispose of the aluminium dust left after firing carefully, wearing a respirator to avoid breathing it in.

THE SOLUTIONS

Contain the aluminium after firing: Pack the individually wrapped pots into a pre-fired container made from grogged clay and place it inside the kiln. All the remnants can then be lifted out and disposed of easily at the end of the firing.

How to use aluminium foil saggars:

1 Lay the clay item on a bed of fine sawdust and pack it around with other combustible materials such as seaweed, banana skins, leaves, grasses and so on.
2 Experiment by adding rock salt, damp paper, fabric, string, wire or whatever you think may make an interesting mark. Oxides will not volatize below 800°C (1482°F), so unless you are firing higher than this, there is no point including any in the mix.
3 Scrunch one layer of aluminium foil around the form, then encase it in a second layer.
4 Fire the work rapidly up to 700°C (1292°F), then remove it from the kiln with tongs and open to see what has happened. Fire again if not satisfied and experiment by firing at different rates to different temperatures up to 800°C (1472°F) – for example, 600°C (1112°F) in six minutes, 700°C (1292°F) in seven minutes. Speed up or slow down the firings according to the results – some experimentation is required.

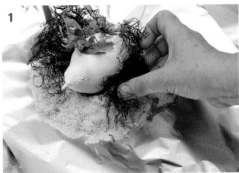

Alternative packing
■ Pack the saggars inside a plant pot placed inside the kiln. Place a kiln shelf over the top to contain any dust.

■ Use a plant pot as an alternative saggar to foil. It should be thoroughly dry before firing; heat it slowly in the raku kiln to eliminate any moisture. Allow it to cool before packing it with sawdust and pots and seal with a kiln bat as before.

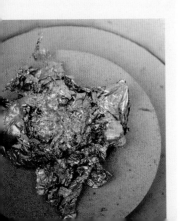

Applying white on white

THE PROBLEM

Difficulty applying resist raku slip and glaze

Difficulty knowing which areas have and have not been covered. In addition, both glaze and slip bubble up when being applied, which later manifests as black dots on the surface of the pot.

Caused by: Both slip and glaze are white, making it hard to distinguish between them. Bubbling occurs when secondary layers of slip or glaze are applied over a previous dry layer as moisture seeks to escape.

THE SOLUTIONS

Stain the resist slip: Use a food colour such as cochineal – it will burn away in firing. The colour difference makes it easy to see which areas have already been covered.

Dip in slip: Dip the pot in the resist slip to avoid creating air bubbles by overworking areas when brushing.

Spray the glaze over the slip: This will prevent prolonged brush contact, which is inclined to cause bubbling. If brushing is the only option, load the brush and apply quickly, trying not to overwork an area. If bubbles form, do not be tempted to fill them in with glaze – it will go through the slip layer and fire onto the pot!

Fire the kiln a little higher: If the glaze has a good melt, it will go some way towards minimizing the bubble effect.

It is easy to see the difference between slip and glaze when one is dyed a colour.

Raku resist glaze issues

THE PROBLEM

Resist raku glaze sticks

After firing, the glaze (which should shell away easily) is hard to remove.
Caused by: The slip layer being too thin, allowing the glaze and the clay surface to fuse; the slip not containing enough quartz; the firing being too high, fusing the glaze despite the resist layer; the glaze layer being too thick and so forming a hard shell.

THE SOLUTIONS

Induce thermal shock: Transfer the pot to a narrow metal bucket while it is still hot and sprinkle with water – the thermal shock should encourage the glaze to crack and break away.

Even coverage: Make sure that the resist slip is at least 3mm (⅛ in) thick and evenly covers the form.

Resist slip recipe: Use three parts china clay to two parts flint or quartz – it should be the consistency of single cream.

Melt the glaze: The actual temperature is not crucial when resist raku firing, but the glaze must melt to be successful. Somewhere between 850 and 925°C (1562 and 1697°F) is optimal. Lift the work out of the kiln as soon as it appears to melt – just past the point where it bubbles significantly.

Glaze application: Make sure that the glaze layer completely covers the slip layer, but do not apply an over-thick coating. If possible, spray the glaze on to ensure even and adequate coverage.

Transfer the vessel from the reduction bin to a smaller metal bin to avoid over-smoking. Induce thermal shock by sprinkling with water.

Controlling smoke effects

THE PROBLEM

Blurry and sharp smoke effects

Some of the surface smoke marks are well defined and sharp, while others look blurred and softer.

Caused by: The way the form is positioned in the combustible material after firing directly affects smoke effects; the amount of sawdust used.

THE SOLUTIONS

Even smoking: Place sawdust on an old kiln bat with a ring of sand around it. Lift the form out of the kiln and place it on the sawdust, then sprinkle a little more over the top. Quickly place a metal bin over the form so that it is sealed by the sand around the edge. Allow to smoke for the required time.

■ Alternatively, completely cover the form with sawdust in the combustion bin. Leave it in there for only a few minutes for subtle effects, and longer for darker marks. The timing is crucial to the outcome, but experimentation is required.

Avoid thermal shock: Transfer the pot to an empty secondary bin after lifting it from the sawdust to prevent it from thermal shock and cooling too quickly.

It is clear to see where the pot has been sitting in sawdust in the reduction bin as this area has much softer smoke lines than those above where the sawdust did not touch.

Controlling reduction effects

THE PROBLEM

Turquoise glaze looks copper

Instead of coming out of the bin a crazed turquoise colour, the pot looks like beaten copper.

Caused by: Placing the pot in the bin when it is too hot; an intense reduction atmosphere being created when the pot is covered in sawdust and the lid sealed down, thus starving it of oxygen; transferring the pots to the bin too quickly.

THE SOLUTIONS

Smooth transfer: When moving the pot from the raku kiln to the reduction/smoke bin, allow it to cool in the air for a second or two.

Molten glaze: Make sure that the glaze is not still molten when it is put into sawdust. If it is, the surface will be affected and create unsightly marks. Wait a second or two until the glaze looks set.

Even smoking: Instead of covering the entire pot in sawdust, follow the instructions above for an even smoking.

Note: A reduction atmosphere can result from firing copper-rich glazes in the raku kiln if the bung hole is covered up. This will result in a characteristic reduction red glaze, which can also become coppery when further reduced in sawdust.

Lift the pots from the kiln carefully, allowing the wares a moment or two in the air before placing in the reduction bin.

Under-firing raku

THE PROBLEM

Lack of crackle

After firing there is little sign of crackle, the glaze looks pinholed and unglazed areas have not blackened in the smoke as they should.

Caused by: Under-firing; firing items with glaze that melts at different stages in the same firing; lingering too long before transferring the pot to the reduction/smoke bin; the glaze melt point being too high; having too many pots in the kiln, so those last removed have cooled off too much.

THE SOLUTIONS

Don't mix glazes: Fire items with the same glaze in each firing; don't mix glaze types together unless you know categorically that they all melt at the same time.

Monitor firing stages: Observe the glaze through the spy vent as it fires. It will go through several stages, from looking spongy to bubbly, after which the bubbles will soften over and the surface look smooth. This is the time to transfer the pots to the reduction/smoke bin.

Ordered transfer: Move pots to the sawdust-laden reduction/smoke bin in a quick and ordered manner. Have everything ready and at hand before you begin so the process is stress free.

Fire fewer items at a time: This way all works can be lifted out while still hot enough for good smoke effects. Three at a time is a good number if you are working on your own; more if you have help – but be aware that having more than one person emptying a kiln can cause congestion unless you have a really good coordinated system.

Reducing the melting point: If the glaze seems to take forever to melt, you can reduce the melting point by increasing the frit and decreasing the china clay content of the glaze – see the recipe below.

Typical under-fired raku form; the clay body lacks the intense blackness of a properly fired form. The glaze has not melted correctly so is rough and bubbly and shows little sign of crazing, which is the desired effect.

FAILSAFE WHITE CRACKLE GLAZE

It is easy to create a reliable white crackle glaze by simply altering the ingredients by small amounts – try the following recipes and suggestions for colour additions.

RECIPE 1		RECIPE 2	
Alkaline frit	80 parts	Alkaline frit	90 parts
China clay	20 parts	China clay	10 parts
+ Tin oxide	10 parts	+ Tin oxide	10 parts

- The glaze on the left has the higher melting point, but this is simply lowered by changing the proportion of frit – recipe on the right.
  Note: If applying over a white clay body, the glaze does not need the inclusion of tin – the outcome will be white anyway.
- For a clear glaze, omit the tin.
- For coloured glazes, add up to 5 per cent glaze or body stain.
- For shades of blue, add up to 1.5 per cent cobalt oxide.
- For turquoise (in oxidation), add up to 3 per cent copper oxide.
- Other oxides can also be used and are worth experimenting with.
- Include a reduced amount of tin if an opaque coloured glaze is required.

Kilns: packing and firing

Several faults can arise out of packing a kiln badly, many of which have already been referred to in relation to particular failures. Many problems are specific to the kiln type, the fuel used, the method of decoration, and so on. However, there are some generic faults that can be overcome once the cause has been identified.

Support in firing

THE PROBLEM

Slumping

Wares slump over supports such as pins, saddle bars and star stilts.

Caused by: Inappropriate use in high firings – such supports are really only suitable for biscuit and earthenware firings, not clay that has a high shrinkage rate, such as porcelains and stonewares.

THE SOLUTIONS

Making supports: For higher firings and only if really required, try making clay supports from the same body as the pots. These will shrink at the same rate, but are only useful for non-glazed areas.

Silica support
■ Unglazed wares such agate, bone china or porcelain can be supported on silica sand or alumina for both biscuit and high-temperature firings.

■ Place silica sand on the kiln shelf and embed bowls and similar shapes in an inverted position in the sand; this will help keep the shape round.

■ When placing flatwares or dishes, make sure that the silica sand fully supports all of the shape.

Make a dedicated alumina container
1 Make a clay container from grogged high-firing clay for alumina (a fine white powder) to prevent it from displacing in the kiln.

2 Sieve the alumina into the container prior to placing the wares inside.

Firing flatware

THE PROBLEM

Dunting of flatware

Large tiles or other flat items crack in half in firing.

Caused by: Thermal shock – the kiln shelf heats up at a slower rate than the tile on top of it, then retains heat much longer as the tile cools after firing, causing stresses at both stages. With larger items there is even more stress because the wares heat and cool from the outer edges inward. Direct contact with the kiln shelf is, in essence, the cause.

THE SOLUTIONS

Supporting tiles: Use saddles (triangular section bars) so that tiles no longer sit directly on the kiln shelf. Use lots randomly positioned as shown. Similarly, support the tile for secondary firings in the same way.

The wall panel has fired successfully simply by being elevated from the kiln shelf by the saddle bars.

■ Make slabbed strips to fire the tiles on. Roll out a slab of clay, cut into strips up to 2 cm (¾ in) thick and either biscuit fire first or biscuit fire the tile and strips together in situ. A little alumina dusted over the strips will stop them sticking to the underside of the tile; the strips will elevate the tile, but shrink at the same rate.

Kiln space saving

THE PROBLEM

Lack of space

Tiles stacked on top of one another during biscuit firing in order to maximize space crack and dunt.

Caused by: Thermal shock: clay at the outer rims of the tiles and those at the top or bottom of the pile heat and cool faster than those in the middle of the stack; weight: the weight of clay is too great, causing the tiles to shrink and consequently fire unevenly, thus causing excess stress.

THE SOLUTIONS

Clay support: To biscuit fire, stack tiles vertically on a kiln shelf, separating them with one or two small wads of clay and using kiln props as supports at each end.

Many tiles can be biscuit fired at a time using this technique.

Use a tile crank: These are available in several sizes and allow many tiles to be fired at a time.

Fusing during firing

THE PROBLEM

Pots stick to the kiln shelf

....

Clay fuses onto the kiln shelf in high firings, even though glaze has not come into contact with the shelf.

Caused by: Lack of a buffer between clay body and kiln shelf, preventing the clay from shrinking as it should – instead, it fuses onto the shelf, often causing the wares to crack in turn; over-firing – firing too high for the clay type or soaking for too long.

The glaze has clearly run off of this form, fusing it to the kiln shelf. If you are unsure of whether or not the glaze will run, it would be best to place the form on old sections or shards of kiln shelf. This way old, broken shelves can be put to good use and good shelves saved from potential damage.

THE SOLUTIONS

Prevent wares sticking to kiln shelves: Paint the kiln shelves with bat wash – a 50/50 mixture of china clay and alumina mixed with water to the consistency of single cream. After firing, the wash will harden on the shelves and prevent many things from sticking.

■ Spread a thin layer of silica sand on the kiln shelf. The tiny particles of sand will act like ball bearings, allowing the clay to move as it shrinks in firing and preventing it from coming directly into contact with the kiln shelf. Take care not to allow grains of sand to fall onto shelves below because they will fire into glaze and be visible as horrible little specks.

Clay suitability: Make sure that the clay is suitable for high firings. It is easy to mistake a low-firing white clay for a high-firing one, but the results are usually catastrophic because many low-firing clays will melt and pool onto the shelf if accidentally fired higher. Casting slips are particularly bad.

■ If you use both low- and high-firing clays, devise a method of marking the wares after making so that you can identify what type of firing they require. This way, they won't be mixed up.

Follow the firing range: See page 117 for firing ramps and temperature rates for biscuit and glost. Unless you are particularly aware of a quirk with your kiln that requires a deviation from normal recommendations, follow these guidelines. A deviation of just a few degrees can often be enough to completely change a firing. If experimentation is required, fire to the lower end of the range first, rising by a few degrees in each successive firing to find the optimum for your kiln. Be aware that soaking for too long can cause glaze to run off, in addition to the clay distorting or fusing to the shelf.

Health and safety

Given the breadth of techniques and materials used in ceramics, there are many inherent health and safety issues to consider. Generally, common sense is all that is required to avoid problems, but it helps to be aware of the dangers when planning a workspace.

- The workshop should be well ventilated, with cleanable, impermeable work surfaces and washing facilities close by.
- Never eat, drink or smoke in the workshop.
- Avoid generating airborne dust; clean up regularly using a wet method.
- Avoid brushing up – it makes a dust problem worse. Instead, use a vacuum cleaner with a filter for fine dust.
- Clean up at the end of each working day. Tools and equipment will then be ready for a fresh start the next day.
- Clean up spillages immediately to avoid slippages and prevent drying materials from forming into dust.
- Wear gloves when handling colouring agents and oxides and when mixing glazes and other preparations that may involve toxic ingredients.
- Wear a face/dust mask when mixing glazes or other dry ingredients or powders.
- Wear goggles when fettling or sanding dry or biscuit-fired vessels.
- Wear protective clothing and avoid wiping dirty hands on aprons because dried residue will cause dust.
- Familiarize yourself with the potential dangers of using certain items of machinery and use them consciously with the hazards in mind.
- Site kilns in a separate room or building in a safe place to reduce fire and burn risk.
- Make sure that the area is well ventilated so that fumes can escape during firing.
- Ensure electric kilns are connected by a qualified electrician and have relevant safety control and cut-off switches.
- Keep the kiln area free of combustible materials when the kiln is firing.
- In gas kilns, burners should have safety cut-off valves to prevent gas from entering the kiln when it is not alight.
- Check pipe work and burners on gas kilns regularly to make sure there are no leaks that could cause explosions.
- Be aware that raku firing involves contact with ceramics at very high temperatures: there is high risk of burning. Keep a water supply and a fire extinguisher at hand.
- Make sure there are no trip hazards around the kiln and that safety gear is worn. If several people are firing at the same time, make sure they all know their role in the procedure.
- Keep a first-aid kit at hand.

Glossary

Agateware Clay patterns and structures formed by laminating, mixing or inlaying different coloured clays, to give an effect like agate stone.

Airbrush A device operated with an air compressor used for spraying on colours, either in overall coverage or decorative form.

Alumina (Al_2O_3) Increases glaze viscosity, firing range and resistance to crystallization.

Alumina hydrate – ($Al(OH)_3$) An alumina source rarely used in clay bodies or glazes but for kiln shelf wash, wadding and in a granular form as a placing sand for firing delicate items and bone china. Small additions increase the viscosity of glaze melt but should not be used as a matting agent because it produces immature glaze – not suitable for functional glazing.

Ash Useful ingredient as the fluxing agent for a glaze. Wood ash is usual, but coal ash, and any plant ash, is also usable. Ash also may have a high silica content, and combined with clay it will form a simple stoneware glaze.

Ball clay Clay of high plasticity, high firing and pale in colour. An ingredient of throwing clay and other bodies, as well as glazes.

Ball mill An enclosed, revolving cylinder containing flint or porcelain balls that are used to grind ceramic oxides or materials mixed with water.

Banding wheel A turntable operated by hand, used for decorating purposes.

Barium carbonate – Poisonous. A secondary flux in stoneware and porcelain glazes – produces vellum matt. Up to 2.5% can be added to some clay bodies to prevent scumming arising from soluble salts.

Bat A plaster or wooden disk for throwing pots on, moving pots without handling or for drying clay.

Bat wash Also a term for kiln wash.

Beating Also a term for paddling.

Bentonite A plastic volcanic clay used in small amounts for suspending glazes or increasing the plasticity of a clay body.

Biscuit (bisque) Clayware after the first firing, usually around 1000°C (1830°F). First, low-temperature firing to which a pot is subjected. Moisture within the clay is driven off slowly in the form of steam, along with other organic compounds – clay becomes converted to 'pot', a chemical change that is irreversible. Biscuit firing is usually between 850°C and 1000°C (1562°F and 1832°F) but can be higher if less porosity is required. Work is often biscuit fired before being decorated.

Biscuit firing The first firing of pottery to mature the clay, rendering it permanent. In a biscuit firing, pots may be stacked on or inside each other because there is no glaze to stick them together.

Blunger High-speed mechanical mixer for slip, usually casting slip.

Body The term used to describe a particular mixture of clay, such as a stoneware body and porcelain body.

Body/clay body Term potters use for clay, especially when it is a prepared mixture and may contain other nonplastic materials such as grog and sand.

Bone china A clay body with a quantity of bone ash in the recipe.

Borax – Toxic. A vigorous low-temperature glaze flux. Slightly soluble in water so usually introduced to glazes as a frit.

Burnishing Compacting a clay surface or slip coating by rubbing in the leather-hard state with a smooth, hard object to give a polished finish.

Calcine A form of purifying by heating oxides or compounds to drive out carbon gases or water and to reduce plasticity in powdered clays.

Calcium chloride Used as a flocculent in glazes having the effect of allowing the glaze constituents to settle in a loosely packed arrangement thus making them more easily reconstituted. Mix the flocculent in a cup with hot water until no more can be dissolved. Allow to cool then mix only a few drops per litre/pint of glaze and mix thoroughly. Larger additions will cause the glaze to thicken – useful when applying the glaze to vitreous wares.

Carborundum stone A hard, dense stone that is used for grinding away rough patches on fired ceramic.

Casting Making pots by pouring slip into a porous mould to build up a layer of clay.

Casting slip A liquid clay used in the process of forming objects with moulds. Also referred to simply as slip.

Celadon Green stoneware and porcelain glaze colours, which contains iron.

Ceramic Any clay form that is fired in a kiln.

Chattering An irregular surface caused by blunt turning tools or a coarse grog in the clay.

China A term associated with vitreous white wares and porcelain.

China clay A pure nonplastic primary clay, used in bodies and glazes.

Christobalite – Hazardous if inhaled. A powdered, prefired form of silica used to improve craze resistance of slips and bodies.

Chuck A hollow clay or plaster form that holds a pot securely during trimming.

Chum A metal turning lathe attachment for placing leather-hard hollow ware over to hold it while turning. Also applies to a turned dome of clay, over which leather-hard articles are placed, prior to turning.

Chun Chinese glaze which gives a milky blue colouring when fired.

Clay ($Al_2O_3.2SiO_2.2H_2O$) Essentially the product of weathered granite and feldspathic rock; a hydrated silicate of aluminium. The purest 'primary' clay, china clay (kaolin), is found where it was formed. Transported 'secondary' clays become contaminated, are coloured and, due to the variable presence of fluxes, have a range of lower firing temperatures.

Clay body A balanced blend of clay, minerals and other nonplastic ingredients that make up the pottery structure.

Cobalt oxide/carbonate (CoO and $CoCO_3$) Powerful blue colourants. Used widely in ancient China, cobalt is said to have been first found in Persia. Blue and white decoration is one of the strongest traditions in ceramics.

Coiling Forming using coils.

Colemenite (boro–calcite) A useful and powerful flux used in glazes to introduce an insoluble form of boron with calcium. Gerstley borate ($2CaO$ $3B_2O_3, 5H_2O$) is a variety of colemenite – used as a flux in studio glazes.

Collaring The action of squeezing around a pot in order to draw the shape inward.

Cones See Pyrometric cones.

Copper oxide/carbonate ($CuCO_3$) Strong colourant in ceramics giving green to black and brown. Under certain reduction conditions it can give a blood red.

Crank Refractory support for tiles, plates, etc. Crank also refers to a type of heavily grogged clay body.

Crawling Movement of glaze over the clay body during the glaze firing, due to dust or grease on the surface.

Crazing The development of fine cracks caused by contraction of a glaze.

Decal Pictures or text printed onto special transfer paper and used to decorate pottery.

Deflocculant An alkaline substance, commonly sodium silicate or soda ash, which when added to a slip, makes the mixture more fluid without the addition of water. The clay particles remain dispersed and in suspension, an essential quality required for casting. Also see Flocculant.

Deflocculation The dispersion of clay slip or glaze by the addition of an electrolyte – e.g., sodium silicate or soda ash – thereby increasing fluidity and decreasing thixotropy.

Dipping Applying a glaze by immersion.

Dolomite A naturally occurring combination of calcium and magnesium carbonates providing a secondary flux for high-temperature porcelain and stoneware glazes.

Downdraught kiln One in which heat and flames are drawn downward and out through flues at the base or floor of the kiln.

Dunting Cracking of pottery due to a too rapid cooling after firing.

Earthenware Pottery fired to a relatively low temperature. The body remains porous and usually requires a glaze if it is to be used for containing water or food. Low temperature ceramics are generally fired between 1000°C and 1180°C (1832°F and 2156°F). Earthenware pottery is fused but not vitrified and remains porous unless covered with a glaze. Naturally occurring red terracotta clays have a relatively high iron oxide content that acts as a flux and therefore will not withstand high temperatures. White earthenware is a manufactured clay body used for industrial production.

Egyptian paste A highly alkaline body with low plasticity and alumina content. The alkali comes to the surface in drying, leaving crystals that flux in firing to give a glazed surface. Colouring oxides are also added to the body.

Enamels Low-temperature colours containing fluxes, usually applied on top of a fired glaze. Enamels require a further firing to render them permanent. Also known as on-glaze colours or china paints.

Engobe A white or coloured slip applied to pottery before glazing. Usually the slip contains an amount of flux to fire it onto the biscuit pot.

Feldspar A common and naturally occurring mineral used as the major flux in clay bodies and in high-temperature glazes. Potash felspar (orthoclase) is the most commonly used form of feldspar. Soda feldspar (albite) is another form of feldspar.

Fettling The process of cleaning up slip-cast pottery with a knife or sponge, especially when removing seams left by a mould.

Filter press Machine into which slip is pumped under pressure so that water is extracted, leaving a stiff plastic clay.

Fireclay Refractory clay used as an additive to stoneware bodies to produce an open texture and speckling (under reduction).

Firing The process by which ceramic ware is heated in a kiln to bring glaze or clay to maturity. Process that changes clay to ceramic (see Biscuit). The usual firing ranges referred to are raku, the lowest at around 800°C (1472°F), followed by earthenware, then stoneware, and finally porcelain, which can be fired up to a maximum of 1400°C (2552°F).

Firing chamber The interior of the kiln in which pottery is fired.

Firing cycle The gradual raising and lowering of the temperature of a kiln to fire pottery.

Flange The rim on the inside of a lid and the ledge around the inside of a pot's opening that are used to locate the lid and hold it securely in place. The ledge on which the lid sits is sometimes called a gallery.

Flint – Hazardous if inhaled. A refractory material used to provide silica in bodies and glazes. Increases firing temperature and craze resistance but reduces plasticity and shrinkage.

Flocculant An acid or salt, which when added to slip has a thickening effect and aids suspension, delaying settlement. Calcium chloride and vinegar are commonly used flocculants.

Flocculation The aggregation of suspended particles by the addition of electrolytes – e.g., calcium chloride – to give a proper consistency for dipping, casting, etc. Flocculation decreases fluidity and increases thixotropy.

Flux An ingredient in a glaze or clay that causes it to melt readily, helping silica to form glaze or glass.

Food-safe Pottery or glaze that has been tested and determined to be safe for use with food or drink.

Foot The base of a piece of pottery on which it rests.

Foot ring The circle of clay at the base of a pot that raises the form from the surface it is standing on.

Frit Glaze ingredients that have been fused to give a more stable substance and to render harmless any dangerous material. Most lead compounds have been fritted to prevent the release of lead into food or drink.

Fused Melted together, but not necessarily vitrified.

Fusion When the fluxes in a body cause the clay to melt and form a solid composition.

Gallery See Flange.

Glaze A thin, glassy layer on the surface of pottery.

Glaze fit How well a fired glaze adheres to the clay body. Ideally, the glaze should have a slightly lower thermal expansion than the body, so that on contraction the body puts the glaze into compression. This avoids glaze crazing due to stresses.

Glaze stain Commercial colour added to a glaze.

Glost Alternative word for glazed, more commonly used in industry.

Greenware Unfired clay ware.

Grog A ceramic material, usually clay, that has been heated to a high temperature before use. Usually added to clay to lessen warping and increase its resistance to thermal shock.

Ground-laying Applying an even coat of enamel with an oil medium to a once-fired glaze surface and refiring to a low temperature of approximately 750°C (1350°F).

Gum arabic and gum tragacanth Water-soluble gums, used as adhesive in glaze or colours.

Glossary

Hardening on Heating decorated biscuit pottery to a temperature of approximately 650–700°C (1200–1290°F) in order to burn out the organic media of the decoration and to fix the colour prior to glazing.

Heat work Energy input during firing, normally represented in terms of temperature and time.

Hot spot A section of a kiln that fires to a hotter temperature than the rest of the kiln.

Incise The process of carving a design into a raw clay surface.

Inglaze To apply pigment, stain or glaze to an unglazed or glazed surface so that in subsequent firings the colour melts into, and combines with, the glaze layer.

Iron oxide The most common and very versatile colouring oxide, used in many slips and glazes and often present in clays too. Red iron oxide (rust) is the most usual form but there are others (black iron, purple iron, yellow ochre).

Kaolin China clay. Primary clay in its purest form ($Al_2O_3.2SiO_2.2H_2O$).

Kidneys See Ribs and Scrapers.

Kiln The device in which pottery is fired. Kilns can be fuelled with wood, oil, gas or electricity.

Kiln furniture Refractory pieces used to separate and support kiln shelves and pottery during firing.

Kiln setting The way in which a kiln is packed for firing.

Kiln wash A coating of refractory material applied to kiln furniture to prevent it from sticking during firing.

Kneading A method of de-airing and dispersing moisture uniformly through a piece of clay to prepare it for use. Sometimes referred to as wedging.

Lead release The amount of lead that can be dissolved from the surface of a glaze that has been in contact with acidic solutions.

Lead sesquisilicate A high lead content frit with low solubility in weak acid or water.

Leather hard Clay that is stiff but still damp. It is hard enough to be handled without distorting but can still be joined.

Lithium carbonate An alkaline flux used as a substitute for potash or soda where a good craze resistance is

required. It provides an alkaline colour response.

Lug Side projection of a pot that acts as a handle for lifting.

Lustres Salts of metals fired at low temperatures, giving a lustrous or iridescent metallic sheen to a body or glaze surface.

Luting The blending of two clay surfaces, using slip.

Magnesium sulphate (Epsom salts) Used to flocculate glazes to assist suspension and application to more vitreous wares.

Majolica Decorated tin-glazed earthenware with the colour decoration being applied on top of the raw glaze surface.

Matt A soft finish with little or no shine.

Matting agent Ceramic compound used to give matt surfaces when added to glazes.

Maturing temperature The temperature at which a clay body develops the desirable hardness, or glaze ingredients fuse into the clay body.

Melting point When a clay, in firing, fuses and turns to a molten glasslike substance.

Mini bars Pyrometric bars used to measure the firing temperature of a kiln. They are usually used in a kiln sitter, a mechanical device that shuts off power to the kiln when the bar has bent enough to release a weighted switch.

Mochaware Type of decoration performed at the wet slip stage when a mixture of alkaline liquid and pigment rapidly disperses into the slip giving a fine lattice pattern.

Mould A plaster former in which clay can be pressed or slip cast to create forms. Moulds can be made up of only one section or multiple pieces.

Mould strap (mould band) A band made of cloth or, more commonly, rubber used to secure parts of a mould together during the pouring process.

Muffle Refractory chamber inside a fuel-burning kiln that contains the pottery and protects it from direct contact with the flames and gases.

Nepheline syenite A mineral mixture of feldspar and hornblende with a little silica. More fusible than feldspar, it can

be used as a replacement to reduce the maturing range of glazes and bodies

Nesting Stacking pottery in a kiln for biscuit firing. Pots can safely be placed inside one another.

Once firing Firing ceramics without a biscuit firing, usually with a raw glaze or pigment applied at the leather-hard or dry stage.

On-glaze colour See Enamels.

Opacifier Material used to make a glaze more opaque, often tin oxide, titanium oxide or zirconium silicate.

Opaque Glazes that do not allow other colours to show through, as opposed to transparent glazes.

Oxidation Firing pottery in a kiln with sufficient supplies of oxygen.

Paddling Tapping a wooden tool against a piece of clay to alter its shape.

Peeling A defect in glazed pottery where the engobe or glaze separates from the body in flakes, usually due to high compression stresses in the layer.

Pinholes A glaze or body fault caused by trapped air erupting through the body or glaze during firing.

Plaster of Paris/plaster ($2CaSO_4.H_2O$) A semi-hydrated calcium sulphate, derived from gypsum by driving off part of the water content. Used in mould making.

Plastic clay Clay that can be manipulated, but still retains its shape.

Porcelain Highly vitrified white clay body with a high kaolin content. Developed in ancient China, its low plasticity makes it a difficult clay to work with. It can be fired as high as 1400°C (2552°F) and when thinly formed, the fired body is translucent.

Pouring hole The opening of the mould used for pouring the slip into the mould cavity.

Primary clays Those clays that have remained in their forming grounds, such as china clay or kaolin.

Prop A refractory clay pillar used for supporting kiln shelves during firing. Also known as posts.

Pugging Mixing and extruding clay from a pug mill.

Pug mill Machine for mixing and extruding plastic clay.

Pyrometer An instrument for measuring the temperature inside a kiln chamber. Works in conjunction with a probe (thermocouple) placed through a hole drilled through the top or side of the kiln wall.

Pyrometric cones Small pyramids made of ceramic materials that are designed to soften and bend when a particular ratio of temperature and time is reached during firing.

Quartz – Hazardous if inhaled. A form of silica used as an alternative to flint in glazes but not an exact alternative to flint in clay bodies.

Raku A firing technique in which pots are placed directly into a hot kiln and removed when red-hot.

Raw glazing See Single fired.

Reactive glaze One that combines with a harder glaze when fired under or over it.

Reducing atmosphere Deficiency of free oxygen in a kiln atmosphere that causes the reduction of compounds rich in oxygen, which affects the glaze and clay colour.

Refractory Ceramic materials that are resistant to high temperatures. Kiln bricks and shelves are made from refractory materials.

Resist A decorative medium, such as wax, latex or paper, used to stop slip or glaze from sticking to the form's surface.

Ribs Wooden or plastic ribs are tools used to lift the walls of thrown pots, while rubber ribs are used for compacting and smoothing clay surfaces. Some ribs are kidney shaped and may be referred to as kidneys.

Rutile An ore containing titanium dioxide with iron oxide used to produce a mottled buff brown colour (3–8%) especially in the presence of ilmenite. Increases the opacity of glaze and exciting effects can be achieved in combination with stains or colouring oxides.

Salt glaze A glaze formed by introducing salt into a hot stoneware kiln.

Saggar A box made from fire clay used for holding glazed pots in a fuel-burning kiln to protect the pots from direct contact with the flames and gases.

Sawdust firing Sawdust is the fuel most often used for smoking or reducing ceramics at low temperatures.

Secondary (residual) clays Primary clays that have been carried away by erosion and earth movements and have combined, in the process, with mineral impurities.

Scrapers Thin metal and plastic tools used to refine clay surfaces. They may be either straight or kidney shaped, and are sometimes referred to as ribs or kidneys respectively.

Seam lines Small lines on pottery produced where two sections of a mould join or where sides come together in slab construction.

Semimatt A satin-like surface that has a slight sheen to it.

Semiopaque Colours that generally allow only dark colours to show through.

Semitransparent Slightly coloured and/or speckled colours that allow most colours to show through with only slight distortions.

Sgraffito The cutting or scratching through an outer coating of slip, glaze or engobe to expose the different coloured body beneath. From the Italian word 'graffito', meaning to scratch.

Silica/silicon dioxide (SiO_2) Primary glass-forming ingredient used in glazes and also present in clay. Silica does not melt until approximately 1800°C (3272°F) and must always be used in conjunction with a flux to reduce its melting point to a workable temperature range.

Silica sands Usually available in several grades. Used as a grog for clay bodies or as a placing sand for firing.

Single fired The making, glazing and firing of pottery in a single operation. Also known as raw glazing.

Slab building Making pottery from slabs of clay.

Slip Liquid clay.

Slip casting Casting slip is made from clay and water, but also contains a deflocculant, allowing a reduced water content. Poured into a plaster mould, casting slip is then left to build up a shell on the inside of the mould before pouring out the excess. Remaining moisture is absorbed by the plaster.

Slip trailing Decorating with slips squeezed through a nozzle.

Soak Keeping a predetermined temperature at the end of the firing cycle to maintain the level of heat in the kiln to enhance many glaze finishes.

Spacers Hollow sections of a thin-walled clay cylinder, used to glue pieces of pottery together.

Spare The section of a model that will form the pouring hole when casting a plaster mould.

Sponging Cleaning the surface of pottery before firing or a decorative method of applying slip or glaze.

Sprigging Plastic clay applied to an article to form a relief decoration.

Spy holes (vent holes) Small holes in the door or side of a kiln used for viewing cones and ventilating the kiln during firing.

Stains Unfired colours used for decorating pottery or a ceramic pigment used to add colour to glazes and bodies.

Stilts Small shapes of biscuit clay, used for supporting glazed pottery during firing.

Stoneware Vitrified clay, usually fired above 1200°C (2190°F). Any glaze matures at the same time as the body, forming an integral layer.

Talc/French chalk/magnesium/ silicate/soapstone A secondary flux introducing magnesium and used to improve craze resistance in glazes – also a flux for clay bodies.

Temperature conversion table
To convert °F into °C – Deduct 32, multiply by 5 and divide by 9.
To convert °C into °F – Multiply by 9, divide by 5 and add 32.

Terracotta An iron-bearing earthenware clay that matures at a low temperature and fires to an earth-red colour.

Terra sigillata A very fine slip used as a surface coating for burnishing or other decorative treatments.

Thermal expansion The expansion that occurs in glazes and clays during firing.

Thermal shock Sudden expansion or contraction that occurs in a clay or glaze and causes damage, usually through sudden heating or cooling.

Thermocouple The temperature probe in a kiln that transmits information to the pyrometer.

Thixotropy The ability of clay suspensions to thicken up on standing. See also Deflocculation and Flocculation.

Throwing Clay is placed on a rotating potter's wheel and formed by hand in conjunction with centrifugal force. Wheel designs vary from momentum 'man-powered' wheels, through pedal type 'kick wheels' and belt-driven, hand-turned arrangements to the modern highly powered electric version. Throwing is said to have been developed first in Egypt c. 3000 BC.

Tin oxide The oldest and most widely used opacifier producing a soft white. Add 5–10% for opacification.

Titanium dioxide A cream-white opacifier often used as a constituent of vellum glazes.

T material Highly grogged white plastic clay.

Toxic Any ceramic material, raw, gaseous or liquid, that is injurious to health.

Transparent Clear base colours that are free from cloudiness and distortion.

Tube line To decorate on a fired or unfired clay body, giving a raised line. The tube line is a mixture of clay, flux and other ceramic compounds.

Turning Trimming thrown pots in the leather-hard state to refine their shape and to create foot rings.

Twaddell degrees (°TW) Units used to measure the specific gravity of solutions and suspensions.

Updraught kiln A fuel-burning kiln in which the smoke goes into and through the kiln and up the chimney.

Under-firing Not firing hot enough or long enough, or both.

Underglaze A colour that is usually applied to either greenware or biscuit-fired pottery and in most cases is covered with a glaze. A medium, such as gum arabic, is usually used to adhere the colour to biscuit but needs to be fired on before glazing.

Vitrification point The point at which clay particles fuse together.

Vitrified Usually refers to porcelain and stoneware that are fired at a high temperature. The clay begins to become glasslike.

Volatilize To become vapourous. Certain oxides, such as copper, do this at high temperatures and are deposited onto other pots and kiln shelves.

Volume calculations The volume of an object can be measured using displacement. When immersed in water, a solid object will displace its own volume in water. With the help of measuring cylinders you will be able to calculate its volume.

Volume (v) of a cylinder
Volume = $\pi r2 h$ (in which π = pi or 3.142; r = radius; h = height)
Volume = 3.142 x r x 2 x h

Volume of a block
Volume = l x b x h (in which l = length; b = breadth; h = height)

Volume of a cone
Volume = ⅓ $\pi r2 h$ (in which π = pi or 3.142; r = radius; h = height)

Wad box A manually operated machine for extruding cross-sections of clay.

Wedging A method of preparing plastic clay by distributing clay particles and additives such as grog evenly throughout the clay mass.

Wheel head The circular revolving flat disk, attached to the potter's wheel, and on which the pot is thrown or formed.

Whiting/chalk/limestone/calcium carbonate The main source of calcium in glazes and extensively used as a flux in stoneware and porcelain glazes. Assists hardness and durability and in large quantities produces mattness.

Wollastonite/calcium silicate An alternative to whiting as a source of lime in stoneware glazes. Useful where pinholing is a problem.

Zircon (zirconium zilicate) An ultra-fine form of zircon used as an opacifier. Add 5–8% for semiopaque and 10–15% for fully opaque glazes.

Index

A

agate surface protection 109
agate warps and bloats 108
air in the clay 9, 12, 53, 54, 74

B

ball clays 36, 37, 38
bittiness 24
black clay, chunky 45
   smooth 45
black spot 29
blackening 28
blistering 20, 24, 103
bloating 20, 24, 104, 108
blow out 19
bone china 50
   black spot 29
   plastic bone china recipe 50
boulder clay 37
brittle casts 15
Brongniart's formula 65
bulging clay surface 69
burnishing 101
burrs 100

C

casting slips 40
   lumps in the casting slip 85
casting spot 15
casts
   flabby casts 15
   laminated casts 15
chattering 82
china clay 36
   conversion of feldspar to china clay 37
chittering 22, 81
chrome green glaze firing pink 27
clay 34
   ageing clay 40
   clay bodies 38
   clay processing 40
   conversion of feldspar to china clay 37
   conversion of feldspar to clay 35
   earthenware clays 38
   porcelain bodies 39
   primary or residual clays 34
   secondary or sedimentary clays 34–35
   stoneware clays 39
clay particle orientation 41
   problems 41
clay problems
   air in the clay 9, 12

clay not plastic enough 9, 55
clay too dry 9, 55
clay too plastic 9
clay too wet 9, 54
   fungal growth in or on clay 10
   low green strength 16
   scumming 16
   specking 16
clay types 42
   black clays 45
   bone china 50
   paper clays 51
   porcelain 48–49
   stonewares 46–47
   terracotta 42–44
   white earthenware 45
coiling 59
   collapsing shape 69
   lumpy, bulging clay surface 69
collapsing forms 12, 23, 74
collapsing shape 11, 69
collaring in collapse 75
colour 96, 97
   bubbly or frizzled overglaze colours 28
   chrome green glaze firing pink 27
   colour changes in overglaze decoration 29
   colour changes in underglaze decoration 29
   colour transfer 27
   colour variations 24
   lustre colour 29, 109, 110
   milky-looking underglaze colour 28
   patchy colour 24
   recipes for coloured clay 108
   turquoise glaze looks copper 131
combustibles 119
   difficulty getting combustibles to
      burn 126
conversions 94
crackle 132
cracks 70
   cracks in slip-cast wares 18
   rim cracks 18, 79, 81
   spiral cracks 19
   surface cracks 18
cratering 32
crawling 25, 28, 106
crazing 26, 105
cross-draught kilns 115

D

decals 29, 110
diagnostic charts 8–33

clay 9–10, 16
clay: hand-building 10–11
clay: slip casting 13–15
clay: throwing 12–13
colouring pigments 27–29
cracks 18–19
drying 17
explosions 19–20
glaze application 22–23
glaze faults in fired surfaces 23–27
glaze preparation 21
inside the kiln 33
raku firing 29–33
slips and engobes 21
smoke firing 28
digital programme controllers 117
dimpled glaze 25
dipping 89
distorted shape 11, 68
downdraught kilns 115
draw rings 118
drying 17, 66
   conditions that affect drying 66
   draughts and temperature extremes 66
   drying process in firing 67
   splitting seams 67
   uneven drying 10, 68, 83
   uneven shrinkage 17
   warping 17
dunting 23, 134

E

earthenware 38
   grogged white earthenware 45
   smooth white earthenware 45
electric kilns 114
engobes 21
   blurred pattern when using engobe as
     inlay 102
equipment
   coiling 59
   firing 119
   mould making 63
   pinching 60
   slabbing 62
   slip casting 63
   throwing 61
explosions 32
   bloating and blistering 20
   blow out 19
   general explosions 20
   lime popping 19

low fired strength 20
pinholing 19

F

fat clay 9
feldspar 36
 conversion to clay 37
finger marks 22
fire prevention 127
 smoke firing 128
fireclay 37
firing 114
 elements 118
 heat transmission 118
 low firing 118–119
 measuring temperature 117–118
 Orton pyrometric cone temperatures 120–121
 size and shape of pieces 118
 temperature gradients 118
 tips for low firing 119
 typical biscuit-firing schedule 117
 typical stoneware schedule 117
 what type of kiln? 114–117
 see low firing; raku firing; smoke firing
flaking after firing 98
flaking on biscuit ware 21
flaking on greenware 21
flatware 83, 134
fluxes 91, 92
 frits 93
 proportion of acid and neutral oxides to
  flux 92–93
foot ring, overturned 82
forming 58, 59
 clay preparation 58–59
 coiling 59
 pinching 60
 slabbing 62
 slip casting and mould making 63–65
 throwing 61
frits 93
front-loading kilns 114
fuel-burning kilns 115
fungal growth in or on clay 10

G

gas kilns 115
glaze colouring 96
 chrome green glaze firing pink 27
 colour additions 97
 colour transfer 27
 colour variations 24

patchy colour 24
 turquoise glaze looks copper 131
glaze faults 103
 blistering 24, 103
 bloating 24, 104
 chittered edges 22
 crawling 25, 28, 106
 crazing 26, 105
 dimpled glaze 25
 dunting 23
 finger marks 22
 glaze run off 23, 27, 135
 glaze settlement 21
 glaze too thick 21
 glaze won't adhere to biscuit surface 22
 green glazing 23
 gritty glaze surface 24
 milky glaze 25, 28, 107
 orange peel glaze 25
 paintbrush adheres to surface 22
 peeling 26
 pinholing 26
 raw glazing 23
 specking 27
 starved glaze 107
 trailing 23
 uneven glaze application 22
glaze firing 94
 changes that take place in glaze firing 95
 understanding silica inversions 94
glaze opacity 96
glazing 90
 fluxes 91, 92–93
 glaze composition 92–93
 guidelines 92
 mixing glaze 92–93
green strength 16, 38, 39
grinding 111
gritty glaze surface 24

H

handles 13
 cracking and breaking apart 13
 cracks at base of handles 79
 handles twist 77
health and safety considerations 136

I

inlays 101, 102

J

joins

prominent join marks 15
 splits in joined pinched sections 73

K

kaolin 36
kiln packing 107, 122
 firing flatware 134
 fusing during firing 135
 packing and unpacking the kiln 123
 packing for biscuit firing 122
 packing for glaze firing 122
 space saving 134
 supporting work in the kiln 123, 133
kiln problems
 pots sticking to kiln shelf 27, 33, 135
 uneven firing 33
kilns 114
 cross-draught kilns 115
 digital programme controllers 117
 downdraught kilns 115
 draw rings 118
 electric kilns 114
 front-loading kilns 114
 fuel-burning kilns 115
 gas kilns 115
 oil-fired kilns 116
 paper kilns 116
 pyrometers 118
 pyrometric cones 117
 raku kilns 115
 sawdust kilns 116
 thermocouples 118
 top-loading kilns 114
 updraught kilns 115
 wood-burning kilns 116
kneading 10
 ox-head kneading 53, 58
 spiral kneading 54, 58–59

L

lime popping 19
livering 15
losing centre 81
losing control of shape 70
low firing 118–119
 alternative saggars 129
 applying white on white 130
 cleaning the fired surface 127
 controlling reduction effects 131
 controlling smoke effects 131
 dangers of smoke firing 128
 firing with slip resist 125

Index

preparing the kiln for firing 126
raku resist glaze issues 130
safety when firing 127
under-firing raku 132
working with slip resists 124
lumps in glazes 104
lumps in the casting slip 85
lumpy clay surface 69
lustre 29
gold lustre looks purple 109
inconsistent lustre colour 109

M

machinery 63
masking materials 119
matt overglaze 28
metal leaf application 111
milky glaze 25, 28, 107
mould making 63–65
mould problems
bad seams 85
mould staining 13
mould won't release 13
slip difficult to pour off 14
slip fails to fill the mould 84

O

oil-fired kilns 116
opacity 96
orange peel glaze 25
Orton pyrometric cone temperatures 120–121
overglaze 29
bubbly or frizzled overglaze colours 28
matt overglaze 28
ox-head kneading 53, 58

P

paintbrush adhering to surface 22
pan milling 40
paper clays 51
paper clay filler method 51
paper kilns 116
paper resist 99
peeling glaze 26
peeling slip resist 124
pinching 60
cracking and splitting 70
losing control of shape 70
pinching deep shapes 71
splits in joined pinched sections 73
uneven rims 71

uneven shape 72
pinholing 14, 19, 26, 31, 32
pint weight, measuring 65
plaster work 64
plasticity 9, 36, 37
testing for plasticity 55
porcelain 36, 48
black spot 29
porcelain bodies 39
porcelain casting clay 49
standard porcelain 48
super-white porcelain 49
pots sticking to kiln shelf 27, 33, 135
pouring 89
powdered clay 40
preparation 58–59
clay is too dry 55
clay is too wet 54
firming clay for wedging 52
ox-head kneading 53
reclaiming 52
spiral kneading 54
testing for plasticity 55
wedging 53
pyrometers 118
pyrometric cones 117
Orton pyrometric cone temperatures
120–121

R

raku firing
cratering 32
difficulty applying glaze 31, 130
difficulty applying resists 32, 130
difficulty removing glaze 31, 130
difficulty removing slip 31
explosions 32
glaze fall-off when placing in raku kiln 33
lack of crackle 132
pinhole smoke marks on the surface 31
pinholing 32
uneven firing 33
uneven smoking 32
raku kilns 115
raw glazing 23
reclaiming 52
red clays 37
rims
cracks 18, 79, 81
uneven rims 12, 71, 76
wavy, irregular rims 77

S

safety considerations 136
safety when firing 127
saggars, foil 129
salt glaze 25
sand blasting 111
sawdust kilns 116
scumming 16, 42
seams, bad 85
splitting 10, 67
sgraffito 22
difficulty with inlay pattern 101
messy line definition 100
shivering 26
shrinkage 17
silica inversions 94
slabbing 62
uneven drying 83
slip application methods 89
slip basics 88
slip casting 13–15, 63–65
bad seams 85
brittle casts 15
Brongniart's formula 65
casting spot 15
flabby casts 15
laminated casts 15
livering 15
lumps in the casting slip 85
measuring pint weight 65
mould staining 13
mould won't release 13
pinholing 14
prominent join marks 15
slip difficult to pour off 14
slip fails to fill the mould 84
slow casting 14
wreathing 14, 84
slip housing 40
slips 21
difficulty removing resist slip 30, 31, 127
flaking after firing 98
flaking on biscuit ware 21
flaking on greenware 21
peeling slip resist 124
poor adhesion of slip resist 30, 125
slip bleed under paper resist 99
slumping 133
smoke firing
blurry and sharp smoke effects 131
cracks 30

difficulty removing resist slip 30, 127

poor adhesion of slip resist 30, 125

tannin marks 30

spalling 42

special bodies 40

specking 16, 27

spiral kneading 54, 58–59

spit out 29

splits 70

splits in joined pinched sections 73

splitting seams 10, 67

sponging 89

spraying 89

starved glaze 107

stoneware 39, 46

buff stoneware 46

extra-grogged sculpting stoneware 47

firing schedule 117

grogged stoneware 47

grogged white stoneware 47

pizza body stoneware 47

red-grogged stoneware 46

speckled stoneware 47

wide-firing white stoneware 46

strength

green strength 16, 38, 39

low fired strength 20

surface cracking 11

surface decoration 88

badly fired decal holes 29, 110

blackening 28

bubbly or frizzled overglaze colours 28

colour and opacity in glazes 96–97

colour application 27

colour changes in overglaze decoration 29

colour changes in underglaze decoration 29

decorating faults 108–110

glaze crawl 28

glaze faults 103–107

glazing 90–95

last resort solutions 111

lustre colour not firing true 29, 109, 110

matt overglaze 28

methods of slip application 89

milky-looking underglaze colour 28

poor surface finish 109

porcelain and bone china black spot 29

slip and engobe faults 98–102

slip basics 88

spit out 29

underglaze blur 28

T

tannin marks 30

teapot spouts 13

cracking and breaking apart 13

teapot spout twists in firing 78

terracotta 37, 42

fine terracotta 43

grogged terracotta 44

moulding clay terracotta 44

sculpture terracotta 43

scumming 42

spalling 42

standard terracotta 43

thermocouples 118

throwing 12–13, 61

air in clay 74

collapsing forms 74

collaring in collapse 75

cracks at rim and base of handles 79

cracks in the base of thrown forms 80

handles twist 77

rim cracks 81

teapot spout twists in firing 78

uneven walls and rims 76

wavy, irregular rims 77

tiles 83, 134

tools

coiling 59

firing 119

machinery 63

miscellaneous tools 63

mould making 63

pinching 60

slabbing 62

slip casting 63

throwing 61

top-loading kilns 114

trailing 23

turning

chattering 82

losing centre 81

overturned foot ring 82

turquoise glaze looks copper 131

U

underglaze 29

milky-looking underglaze colour 28

underglaze blur 28

uneven drying 10, 68, 83

uneven firing 32, 33

uneven glaze application 22

uneven rims 12, 71, 76, 77

uneven shape 72

uneven shrinkage 17

uneven smoking 32

uneven walls 11, 12, 76

updraught kilns 115

W

walls, uneven 11, 12, 76

warping 17, 68, 83, 108

wedging 10, 58

air trapped in clay 53

firming clay for wedging 52

wood-burning kilns 116

wreathing 14, 84

Credits

Quarto would like to thank the following artists, agencies and manufacturers for supplying images and materials for this book:

Adar, Andrew, www.axisweb.org/artists/andrewadair,
   Photography: Shannon Toft, p.47t
Cecula, Marek, www.ceculamarek,com,
   Photography: Sebastian Zimmer, p.65
Chiu-i Wu Ceramics, www.chiuiwu.co.uk, p.47b
Clayden, Licy, www.licyclayden.co.uk, p.44b
Daintry, Natasha, www.natashadaintry.com, p.94
Davies, Jo, www.jo-davies.com, p.39t
Dr. Nichols, Gail, Braidwood NSW, Australia,
   www.craftact.org/portfolio/ceramics,
      Photography: Michael Brouet, p.39b
Drysdale, Pippin, www.pippindrysdale.com, p.90
Elms, Fenella, www.fenellaelms.com, p.2
Francois, Reugg, www.francoisruegg.com, p.96t
Heyning, Diederick, HeyningWD Studio,
   www.heyningwd.com, p.49b
Koch, Gabrielle, www.gabrielekoch.co.uk, p.60bl
Lalone, Mike, *Photography:* Brittany McConnell, p.96b
Laverick, Tony, www.tonylaverick.co.uk,
   Photography: Jack Laverick, p.88
Mellor, Angela, www.angelamellor.com, p.50b
Palastanga, Claire, p.48b
Steadman, Barry, www.barrystedman.co.uk, p.44b
Van Hoey, Ann, www.annvanhoey-ceramics.be,
   Photography: Dries Van den Brande, p.38t

Bath Potters' Supplies, p.123br
Unit 18,
Fourth Avenue,
Westfield Trading Estate
Radstock, Nr Bath
BA3 4XE
UK
www.bathpotters.co.uk

The Edward Orton Jr. Ceramic Foundation
6991 Old 3C Highway
Westerville
Ohio, 43082
USA
www.ortonceramic.com

Valentine Clays Limited
The Sliphouse,
18-20 Chell Street,
Hanley,
Stoke-on-Trent
ST1 6BA
UK
www.valentineclays.co.uk

All step-by-step and other images are the copyright of Quarto Publishing plc. While every effort has been made to credit contributors, Quarto would like to apologize should there have been any omissions or errors – and would be pleased to make the appropriate correction for future editions of the book.

Author's acknowledgements

I would like to thank all the makers who have contributed images of their work to this book, but special thanks goes to my good friend Kevin Millward – an oracle for all things ceramic – for his patient advice and help with various sections of the book. Also to those potters who have contributed examples of faults in their work – great potters all of them. I am really grateful that they were willing to show how things can go wrong for even the best makers. They include: Linda Caswell, Mark Dally, Elaine Chassar- Hesketh, Claudia Lis, Ian Marsh, Charmain Poole, Louise Schrempft and my dear friend Chris Mills who is sadly no longer with us.

   Great thanks also to Valentine Clays for supplying clay samples and invaluable information, and finally to Harry Fraser for his diagram of the slip-housing process.